THE HEART HEALTHY COOKBOOK FOR TWO

Quick, Easy and Flavorful Recipes You'll Absolutely Love. Wholesome Cooking for a Happy and Healthy Hearts

ZARA JIMENEZ

TABLE OF CONTENTS

INTRODUCTION

Indulge in the art of culinary exploration and nourishment as you and your partner delve into the delightful world of easy, quick and healthy recipes for two.

This cookbook is a testament to the joy of cooking and eating together, offering a diverse repertoire of nourishing recipes tailored specifically for couples who prioritize heart-healthy living.

Within the pages of this cookbook, you'll find a wealth of delectable dishes designed to elevate your dining experiences while supporting your shared commitment to heart health. From vibrant salads bursting with color and flavor to soul-warming soups, sumptuous main courses, and guilt-free desserts, each recipe is a celebration of the harmonious blend of nutrition and taste.

Embracing a heart-healthy lifestyle doesn't mean compromising on flavor or variety. With this in mind, Heart Healthy Cookbook for Two presents an enticing array of recipes that showcase the versatility and abundance of wholesome ingredients, promising a culinary journey that's both health-conscious and satisfying. Whether you're seeking to create a romantic dinner for two or simply aiming to infuse your everyday meals with nourishing goodness, this cookbook is your gateway to a world of vibrant, heart-healthy flavors.

More than just a collection of recipes, Heart-healthy cookbook serves as a companion on your journey toward wellness and togetherness. It's a guide that encourages you and your partner to revel in the pleasures of preparing and savoring nourishing meals, fostering a deeper connection through the shared experience of creating and enjoying wholesome, heart-healthy cuisine.

Let this cookbook be your trusted ally as you embark on a culinary adventure that nourishes not only your bodies, but also your relationship. Together, revel in the joy of savoring the delightful flavors of a heart-healthy lifestyle, as you and your loved one embrace the art of nourishing your bodies and your bond through the shared love of food.

ABOUT HEART-HEALTHY DIET

A heart-healthy diet is an eating plan designed to promote cardiovascular well-being and reduce the risk of heart disease. It emphasizes the consumption of nutrient-rich foods such as vegetables, fruits, whole grains, lean proteins, and healthy fats, while limiting or avoiding processed foods high in sugar, salt, and unhealthy fats. The overall dietary pattern, rather than individual foods or nutrients, is crucial in supporting heart health. Additionally, heart-healthy diets often include foods rich in omega-3 fatty acids, which can help lower cholesterol levels and reduce the risk of heart disease. By following a heart-healthy diet, individuals can significantly improve their cardiovascular health and overall well-being.

The American Heart Association emphasizes the importance of a heart-healthy dietary pattern, regardless of whether food is prepared at home, ordered in a restaurant, or purchased as a prepared meal. It recommends reading nutrition labels to choose foods with less sodium, added sugars, and saturated fat, and looking for the Heart-Check mark to identify certified heart-healthy foods.

Furthermore, heart-healthy dietary patterns can significantly boost cardiovascular health by influencing aspects such as blood pressure, inflammation, cholesterol levels, and triglycerides. Fruits and vegetables, whole grains, healthy proteins, nonfat and low-fat dairy, and unsaturated fats and oils form the foundation of a heart-healthy eating plan. Conversely, foods high in sodium, saturated fat, added sugars, and alcohol should be avoided to protect heart health.

In summary, a heart-healthy diet is centered around consuming nutrient-dense foods that support cardiovascular well-being while minimizing the intake of foods that can increase the risk of heart disease. By adopting a heart-healthy dietary pattern, individuals can take proactive steps to prioritize their heart health and overall wellness.

HOW TO START HEALTHY DIET

To start a heart-healthy diet, consider the following steps based on expert recommendations and guidelines:

1. Understand the Basics:

Educate yourself about the principles of a heart-healthy diet, including the types of foods to prioritize and those to limit or avoid. Familiarize yourself with the impact of nutrition on heart health and the overall benefits of adopting a heart-healthy dietary pattern.

2. Focus on Nutrient-Rich Foods:

Emphasize the consumption of nutrient-dense foods such as fruits, vegetables, whole grains, lean proteins, and healthy fats. These foods provide essential vitamins, minerals, fiber, and antioxidants that support heart health.

3. Limit Unhealthy Components:

Reduce the intake of processed foods high in sugar, salt, and unhealthy fats. Pay attention to nutrition labels and choose foods with less sodium, added sugars, and saturated fat.

4. Incorporate Heart-Healthy Fats:

Include sources of healthy fats in your diet, such as nuts, seeds, avocados, and certain oils like olive oil. These fats can help lower cholesterol levels and reduce the risk of heart disease when consumed in moderation.

5. Consider the DASH Eating Plan:

Explore the Dietary Approaches to Stop Hypertension (DASH) eating plan, which is highly rated for its heart-healthy benefits. The DASH plan focuses on reducing sodium and saturated fat while emphasizing fruits, vegetables, and whole grains.

6. Seek Professional Guidance:

Consult with your healthcare provider before making significant changes to your diet or exercise routine. They can offer personalized advice, support, and referrals to dietitians or nutritionists for help in planning a heart-healthy diet.

7. Engage in Regular Exercise:

Combine a heart-healthy diet with regular physical activity to further improve blood pressure, cholesterol levels, and overall heart health. Aim for at least 30 minutes of moderate exercise most days of the week, but consult your doctor before starting any new exercise regimen.

8. Create a Meal Plan:

Consider using heart-healthy meal plans as a starting point to jump-start your heart-friendly eating plan. Planning and preparing meals in advance with this cookbook can help you adhere to your heart-healthy dietary goals.

By following these steps, you can lay the foundation for a heart-healthy diet that supports your cardiovascular well-being and overall health. Remember that small, sustainable changes can lead to long-term benefits for your heart and overall well-being.

HOW TO STAY HEALTHY TOGETHER

To maintain a heart-healthy diet for two people, consider the following steps:

1. Educate and Plan Together:

- **Educate Both Partners:**Learn about the principles of a heart-healthy diet together to ensure mutual understanding and commitment.
- **Plan Meals Together:**Collaborate on meal planning to ensure that both partners are actively involved in selecting heart-healthy recipes and ingredients.

2. Emphasize Nutrient-Rich Foods:

- **Prioritize Nutrient-Dense Foods:** Focus on incorporating a variety of nutrient-rich foods such as vegetables, fruits, whole grains, lean proteins, and healthy fats into your shared meals.

3. Limit Unhealthy Components:

- **Avoid Unhealthy Foods:** Together, make a conscious effort to limit or avoid processed foods high in sugar, salt, and unhealthy fats. Support each other in making healthier choices when grocery shopping or dining out.

4. Incorporate Heart-Healthy Fats:

- **Include Healthy Fats:** Integrate sources of healthy fats, such as nuts, seeds, avocados, and certain oils, into your shared meals to promote heart health for both partners.

5. Seek Professional Guidance:

- **Consult Healthcare Providers:** If needed, consult with healthcare providers together to receive personalized advice and support for maintaining a heart-healthy diet as a couple.

6. **Engage in Regular Exercise:**

- **Exercise Together:** Encourage each other to engage in regular physical activity as part of your heart-healthy lifestyle. Consider activities that you both enjoy, such as walking, cycling, or dancing.

7. **Create a Supportive Environment:**

- **Support Each Other:** Foster a supportive environment where both partners encourage and motivate each other to adhere to the heart-healthy dietary plan.

By following these steps together, both partners can actively contribute to maintaining a heart-healthy diet, supporting each other's cardiovascular well-being, and strengthening their shared commitment to a healthy lifestyle.

CHAPTER 1
BREAKFAST

VEGGIE OMELETTE

- Prep Time: 10 minutes
- Cooking Time: 10 minutes
- Servings: 2

Ingredients:

- 4 large eggs
- 1/4 cup milk
- 1/4 teaspoon salt
- 1/4 teaspoon black pepper
- 1 tablespoon olive oil
- 1/4 cup diced onion
- 1/4 cup diced bell peppers
- 1/4 cup diced tomatoes
- 1/4 cup sliced mushrooms
- 1/4 cup chopped spinach
- 1/4 cup shredded cheddar cheese (optional)
- Fresh parsley or chives for garnish (optional)

Directions:

1. In a bowl, whisk together the eggs, milk, salt, and black pepper until well combined. Set aside.
2. Carefully warm the olive oil in a non-stick skillet over a medium heat setting.
3. Start by adding the diced onion and bell peppers into a skillet, ensuring they are evenly spread. Set the heat to medium and allow them to cook for 2-3 minutes. Keep a close eye on them until they start to soften and reach a tender consistency.
4. Next, introduce the tomatoes, mushrooms, and spinach to the skillet. Cook this combination for an additional 2 minutes, ensuring that the vegetables are cooked until they become slightly tender.
5. After cooking the vegetables, proceed by pouring the egg mixture evenly over the cooked vegetables in the skillet. Allow the eggs to cook without disturbance for a brief period, specifically until the edges commence the process of setting.
6. Using a spatula, carefully nudge the cooked edges towards the center, creating space for the uncooked eggs to flow and cook along the edges.

7. Continue the cooking process until the eggs reach a state where they are mostly set, with a slight runniness remaining on the top.
8. If desired, sprinkle the shredded cheddar cheese evenly over the omelette.
9. With the assistance of the spatula, fold the omelette in half, ensuring that all ingredients are enclosed within. Continue to cook the folded omelette for an additional minute, allowing the cheese to melt and the eggs to complete their cooking process.
10. With caution, transfer the omelette to a serving plate and, if desired, embellish it with a garnish of fresh parsley or chives.
11. Cut the omelette in half and serve hot.

Nutritional breakdown per serving:
Calories: 200-250 kcal, Protein: 13 grams, Carbohydrates: 8 grams, Fat: 14 grams, Saturated Fat: 4 grams, Cholesterol: 380 milligrams, Sodium: 400 milligrams, Fiber: 2 grams, and Sugar: 4 grams.

OVERNIGHT CHIA PUDDING

- Prep Time: 5 minutes
- Total Cooking Time: 8 hours (overnight)
- Servings: 2

Ingredients:

- 1/4 cup chia seeds
- 1 cup unsweetened almond milk
- 1 tablespoon maple syrup
- 1/2 teaspoon vanilla extract
- Fresh fruits and nuts for topping (optional)

Directions:

1. In a bowl or jar, bring together the chia seeds, almond milk, maple syrup, and vanilla extract. Carefully and diligently, stir the mixture to guarantee that the chia seeds are evenly spread throughout the entirety of the mixture.
2. Afterward, proceed by covering the bowl or jar and transferring it to the refrigerator. Allow the mixture to sit undisturbed for the duration of the night or a minimum of 8 hours, enabling the chia seeds to absorb the liquid and develop a pudding-like consistency.
3. Once the pudding has solidified, give it a thorough stir to disperse any clumps and ensure that any settled chia seeds are fully incorporated.
4. If desired, divide the chia pudding into serving bowls or jars.
5. Top the pudding with fresh fruits and nuts of your choice, such as sliced strawberries, blueberries, almonds, or shredded coconut.
6. Serve chilled and enjoy!

Nutritional breakdown per serving:

Calories: 160-180 kcal, Protein: 6 grams, Carbohydrates: 16 grams, Fat: 10 grams, Saturated Fat: 1 grams, Cholesterol: 80 milligrams, Sodium: 80 milligrams, Fiber: 10 grams, and Sugar: 4 grams.

SMASHED AVOCADO TOAST

- Prep Time: *5 minutes*
- Total Cooking Time: *5 minutes*
- Servings: *2*

Ingredients:
- 2 ripe avocados
- 4 slices of bread (whole wheat or your preferred bread)
- 1 small garlic clove, minced (optional)
- 1 tablespoon freshly squeezed lemon juice
- Salt and pepper to taste
- Optional toppings: sliced tomatoes, red pepper flakes, microgreens, feta cheese, poached egg, etc.

Directions:
1. To start, halve the avocados, carefully remove the pits, and then scoop out the flesh into a bowl.
2. Utilize a fork to mash the avocados until you attain the desired consistency. If you prefer a smoother texture, consider employing a blender or food processor.
3. Add the minced garlic (if using), lemon juice, salt, and pepper to the mashed avocado. Mix well to combine all the flavors.
4. Toast the bread slices until they reach your desired level of crispness.
5. Take a liberal portion of the mashed avocado mixture and spread it generously onto each slice of toast.
6. Enhance your creation by adding any additional toppings of your preference, such as sliced tomatoes, red pepper flakes, microgreens, feta cheese, or a poached egg.
7. Serve immediately and enjoy!

Nutritional breakdown per serving:
Calories: 250-300 kcal, Protein: 5 grams, Carbohydrates: 33 grams, Fat: 28 grams, Saturated Fat: 4 grams, Cholesterol: 0 milligrams, Sodium: 200 milligrams, Fiber: 10 grams, and Sugar: 2 grams.

GREEK YOGURT PARFAIT

- Prep Time: 10 minutes
- Total Cooking Time: 0 minutes
- Servings: 2

Ingredients:

- 1 cup Greek yogurt
- 1 cup granola
- 1 cup of assorted fresh berries, such as strawberries, blueberries, and raspberries
- 2 tablespoons honey (optional)
- Fresh mint leaves for garnish (optional)

Directions:

1. Begin by dividing the Greek yogurt in half and layering it at the bottom of two serving glasses or bowls.
2. Add a generous layer of granola on the surface of the yogurt.
3. Next, add a layer of mixed fresh berries on top of the granola.
4. Continue the layering process by repeating the sequence with the remaining Greek yogurt, granola, and fresh berries.
5. Drizzle honey over the top of the parfaits, if desired, for added sweetness.
6. To enhance both the flavor and presentation, consider garnishing with fresh mint leaves for an additional burst of taste.
7. Serve immediately and enjoy!

Nutritional breakdown per serving:

Calories: 300-350 kcal, Protein: 15 grams, Carbohydrates: 50 grams, Fat: 8 grams, Saturated Fat: 1 grams, Cholesterol: 5 milligrams, Sodium: 60 milligrams, Fiber: 8 grams, and Sugar: 20 grams.

SPINACH AND MUSHROOM FRITTATA

- Prep Time: 10 minutes
- Total Cooking Time: 25 minutes
- Servings: 2

Ingredients:

- 4 large eggs
- 1/8 cup milk
- 1/8 teaspoon salt
- 1/8 teaspoon black pepper
- 1/2 tablespoon olive oil
- 1/2 cup sliced mushrooms
- 1 cup fresh spinach leaves
- 1/8 cup diced onion
- 2 tablespoons grated Parmesan cheese (optional)
- Fresh herbs for garnish (optional)

Directions:

1. To commence, modify the temperature of your oven to 375°F (190°C).
2. In a bowl, whisk together the eggs, milk, salt, and black pepper until well combined. Set aside.
3. Warm the olive oil in a skillet that is safe for use in the oven, using medium heat.
4. Place the diced onion into the skillet and sauté it for approximately 2-3 minutes, or until it reaches a translucent state.
5. Introduce the sliced mushrooms to the skillet and cook them for an additional 3-4 minutes, or until they begin to soften.
6. Continue the cooking process by adding the fresh spinach leaves to the skillet. Let the spinach leaves cook for an additional minute until they have wilted to the desired consistency.
7. Ensure that the egg mixture is evenly spread over the vegetables in the skillet, covering them entirely. Let it cook without disturbance for approximately 2 minutes, allowing the edges to start setting.
8. If you prefer, you can sprinkle the grated Parmesan cheese evenly over the frittata to add a flavorful finishing touch.

9. Transfer the skillet to the preheated oven and bake for 12-15 minutes until the eggs are fully set and the top is slightly golden.
10. Take the skillet out of the oven and allow it to cool for a few minutes.
11. For an optional finishing touch, consider garnishing with fresh herbs such as parsley or basil.
12. Cut the frittata into triangular portions and serve it while it is still warm.

Nutritional breakdown per serving:

Calories: 150-200 kcal, Protein: 12 grams, Carbohydrates: 4 grams, Fat: 11 grams, Saturated Fat: 3 grams, Cholesterol: 280 milligrams, Sodium: 320 milligrams, Fiber: 1 grams, and Sugar: 1 grams.

QUINOA BREAKFAST BOWL

- Prep Time: 10 minutes
- Total Cooking Time: 20 minutes
- Servings: 2

Ingredients:

- 1 cup cooked quinoa
- 1 cup unsweetened almond milk
- 1 tablespoon honey or maple syrup
- 1/2 teaspoon vanilla extract
- 1/4 teaspoon ground cinnamon
- 1/4 cup chopped nuts
- 1/4 cup fresh berries
- 1 tablespoon chia seeds
- Optional toppings: sliced bananas, shredded coconut, drizzle of nut butter, etc.

Directions:

1. In a saucepan, combine the cooked quinoa, almond milk, honey or maple syrup, vanilla extract, and ground cinnamon.
2. To begin, set the mixture on a stovetop burner at medium heat. Stir it periodically until it reaches a simmering point.
3. Reduce the heat to low and let it cook for 5-7 minutes, stirring occasionally, until the mixture thickens to your desired consistency.
4. Remove the saucepan from the heat and let it cool for a few minutes.
5. Divide the quinoa mixture into two bowls.
6. Top each bowl with chopped nuts, fresh berries, and chia seeds.
7. Customize your dish with additional toppings according to your preferences. Consider options like sliced bananas, shredded coconut, or a drizzle of nut butter.
8. Serve the quinoa breakfast bowls warm.

Nutritional breakdown per serving:

Calories: 300-350 kcal, Protein: 8 grams, Carbohydrates: 45 grams, Fat: 12 grams, Saturated Fat: 1 grams, Cholesterol: 0 milligrams, Sodium: 80 milligrams, Fiber: 8 grams, and Sugar: 12 grams.

BAKED EGG CUPS

- Prep Time: 10 minutes
- Total Cooking Time: 20 minutes
- Servings: 2

Ingredients:

- 4 large eggs
- 2 slices of cooked bacon, crumbled
- 1/4 cup shredded cheddar cheese
- 1/4 cup diced bell peppers
- 1/4 cup diced tomatoes
- 2 tablespoons chopped fresh parsley (optional)
- Salt and pepper to taste
- Cooking spray or butter for greasing

Directions:

1. To commence, modify the temperature of your oven to 375°F (190°C). Grease two wells of a muffin tin with cooking spray or butter.
2. Crack 2 eggs into each greased muffin well, ensuring that the yolks remain intact.
3. Sprinkle the crumbled bacon, shredded cheddar cheese, diced bell peppers, and diced tomatoes evenly over each egg cup.
4. Season with salt and pepper to taste.
5. Next, put the muffin tin into the preheated oven and bake it for 15-18 minutes. Keep an eye on it until the egg whites have set and the yolks have reached your desired level of doneness.
6. After baking, take the muffin tin out of the oven and allow it to cool for a few minutes before handling.
7. Carefully remove the baked egg cups from the muffin tin using a spoon or silicone spatula.
8. Garnish with chopped fresh parsley, if desired.
9. Serve the baked egg cups warm.

Nutritional breakdown per serving:

Calories: 200-250 kcal, Protein: 16 grams, Carbohydrates: 3 grams, Fat: 14 grams, Saturated Fat: 6 grams, Cholesterol: 380 milligrams, Sodium: 400 milligrams, Fiber: 1 grams, and Sugar: 1 grams.

WHOLE-GRAIN PANCAKES

- Prep Time: 10 minutes
- Total Cooking Time: 20 minutes
- Servings: 2

Ingredients:

- 1 cup whole wheat flour
- 1 tablespoon sugar (optional)
- 1 teaspoon baking powder
- 1/2 teaspoon baking soda
- 1/4 teaspoon salt
- 1 cup buttermilk (or 1 cup milk mixed with 1 tablespoon vinegar or lemon juice)
- 1 large egg
- 1 tablespoon melted butter or vegetable oil
- Cooking spray or additional butter for greasing

Optional Toppings:

- Maple syrup
- Fresh berries
- Sliced bananas
- Chopped nuts

Directions:

1. In a large mixing bowl, whisk together the whole wheat flour, sugar (if using), baking powder, baking soda, and salt.
2. To create the batter, take a separate bowl and combine the buttermilk, egg, and melted butter or vegetable oil. Thoroughly whisk the ingredients together until they are fully incorporated and well blended.
3. While stirring, slowly pour the wet mixture into the dry mixture, ensuring that the ingredients are thoroughly combined. Take care not to overmix the batter; it's perfectly acceptable to have a few lumps.
4. After preparing the batter, let it rest for 5 minutes. This will give the whole wheat flour enough time to absorb the liquid and slightly thicken the mixture.

5. Begin by preheating a non-stick skillet or griddle over medium heat. If necessary, lightly coat the surface with cooking spray or butter to prevent sticking.
6. To make each pancake, simply pour 1/4 cup of pancake batter onto the skillet.
7. Allow the pancakes to cook until you notice bubbles forming on the surface and the edges becoming set, which usually takes approximately 2-3 minutes.
8. Once flipped, cook the pancakes for an additional 1-2 minutes until they achieve a golden brown color and are thoroughly cooked.
9. Take the cooked pancakes out of the skillet and ensure they stay warm.
10. Continue the process by repeating steps 6 to 9 with the remaining batter until all the pancakes have been cooked.
11. Serve the whole-grain pancakes with your desired toppings, such as maple syrup, fresh berries, sliced bananas, or chopped nuts.

Nutritional breakdown per serving:

Calories: 250-300 kcal, Protein: 10 grams, Carbohydrates: 37 grams, Fat: 9 grams, Saturated Fat: 4 grams, Cholesterol: 80 milligrams, Sodium: 500 milligrams, Fiber: 5 grams, and Sugar: 6 grams.

BERRY SMOOTHIE BOWL

- Prep Time: 10 minutes
- Total Cooking Time: 5 minutes
- Servings: 2

Ingredients:

- 2 frozen bananas, sliced
- 1 cup frozen mixed berries (such as strawberries, blueberries, and raspberries)
- 1/2 cup unsweetened almond milk
- 1/2 cup plain Greek yogurt
- 1 tablespoon honey or maple syrup (optional)

Toppings:

- Fresh berries
- Sliced bananas
- Granola
- Chia seeds
- Shredded coconut
- Nut butter

Directions:

1. In a blender, combine the frozen bananas, frozen mixed berries, almond milk, Greek yogurt, and honey or maple syrup (if using).
2. Using a high-speed blender, blend the mixture until it becomes smooth and creamy in texture. If needed, add a little more almond milk to achieve your desired consistency.
3. Pour the smoothie mixture into two bowls.
4. Garnish the smoothie bowls with your desired toppings, such as fresh berries, sliced bananas, granola, chia seeds, shredded coconut, or a drizzle of nut butter.
5. Serve the berry smoothie bowls immediately.

Nutritional breakdown per serving:

Calories: 200-250 kcal, Protein: 8 grams, Carbohydrates: 45 grams, Fat: 2 grams, Saturated Fat: 0 grams, Cholesterol: 0 milligrams, Sodium: 60 milligrams, Fiber: 8 grams, and Sugar: 26 grams.

SWEET POTATO HASH

- Prep Time: 15 minutes
- Total Cooking Time: 25 minutes
- Servings: 2

Ingredients:

- 2 medium sweet potatoes, peeled and diced
- 1 small onion, diced
- 1 red bell pepper, diced
- 2 cloves garlic, minced
- 2 tablespoons olive oil
- 1 teaspoon smoked paprika
- 1/2 teaspoon ground cumin
- 1/4 teaspoon chili powder (optional)
- Salt and pepper to taste
- 2 large eggs (optional)
- Fresh parsley or cilantro, chopped (for garnish)

Directions:

1. On the stovetop, set a large skillet over medium heat and heat the olive oil within it.
2. Add the diced sweet potatoes, onion, and red bell pepper to the skillet. While occasionally stirring, cook the mixture for approximately 8-10 minutes until the sweet potatoes become tender and develop a slight golden-brown color.
3. Add the minced garlic, smoked paprika, ground cumin, chili powder (if using), salt, and pepper to the skillet. Thoroughly stir the spices into the sweet potatoes and vegetables, ensuring they are evenly coated. Continue cooking for an additional 1-2 minutes.
4. In the meantime, if desired, fry two eggs in a separate non-stick skillet to serve on top of the sweet potato hash.
5. Divide the sweet potato hash between two plates.
6. If using, place a fried egg on top of each plate of sweet potato hash.
7. Garnish with fresh parsley or cilantro.
8. Serve the sweet potato hash warm.

Nutritional breakdown per serving:

Calories: 300-350 kcal, Protein: 9 grams, Carbohydrates: 45 grams, Fat: 12 grams, Saturated Fat: 2 grams, Cholesterol: 186 milligrams, Sodium: 125 milligrams, Fiber: 8 grams, and Sugar: 12 grams.

BANANA WALNUT MUFFINS

- Prep Time: 15 minutes
- Total Cooking Time: 20-25 minutes
- Servings: 2 (4 muffins)

Ingredients:

- 1 ripe banana, mashed
- 1/4 cup unsalted butter, melted
- 1/4 cup granulated sugar
- 1/4 cup packed light brown sugar
- 1 large egg
- 1/2 teaspoon vanilla extract
- 1/2 cup all-purpose flour
- 1/2 teaspoon baking powder
- 1/4 teaspoon baking soda
- 1/4 teaspoon salt
- 1/4 cup chopped walnuts

Directions:

1. To commence, modify the temperature of your oven to 350°F (175°C). Get ready a muffin tin by either greasing it or placing paper liners in each cup.
2. In a medium-sized mixing bowl, combine the mashed banana, melted butter, granulated sugar, brown sugar, egg, and vanilla extract. Stir until well combined.
3. In another bowl, bring together the flour, baking powder, baking soda, and salt. Use a whisk to thoroughly blend and mix the ingredients until well combined.
4. Blend the wet and dry ingredients together with gentle mixing until they are thoroughly combined. Exercise caution to avoid excessive mixing of the batter, as this can negatively affect the final texture of the dish.
5. Gently fold in the chopped walnuts.
6. Equally distribute the batter among the muffin cups, filling each one approximately two-thirds full.
7. Let the muffins bake in the oven, which has been preheated, for approximately 20 to 25 minutes, or until a toothpick inserted into the center of a muffin comes out clean.

8. After removing the muffins from the oven, give them a brief period to cool down in the muffin tin. Subsequently, transfer the muffins to a wire rack to cool down completely.
9. Serve the banana walnut muffins as a delicious breakfast or snack.

Nutritional breakdown per serving (2 muffins):

Calories: 400-450 kcal, Protein: 6 grams, Carbohydrates: 51 grams, Fat: 21 grams, Saturated Fat: 9 grams, Cholesterol: 98 milligrams, Sodium: 365 milligrams, Fiber: 3 grams, and Sugar: 32 grams.

QUICHE LORRAINE

- Prep Time: 20 minutes
- Total Cooking Time: 45-50 minutes
- Servings: 2

Ingredients:

- 1 refrigerated pie crust (9 inches)
- 4 slices bacon, cooked and crumbled
- 1/2 cup shredded Gruyere cheese
- 1/2 cup shredded Swiss cheese
- 3 large eggs
- 1 cup heavy cream
- 1/4 teaspoon salt
- 1/4 teaspoon black pepper
- 1/8 teaspoon ground nutmeg
- 1 tablespoon chopped fresh chives (optional)

Directions:

1. To initiate the process, adjust the temperature of your oven to 375°F (190°C).
2. Gently position the refrigerated pie crust into a 9-inch pie dish, ensuring a firm press against both the bottom and sides of the dish. Remove any excess crust by trimming it away.
3. In a small mixing bowl, combine the cooked and crumbled bacon, shredded Gruyere cheese, and shredded Swiss cheese. Mix well.
4. Take another bowl and combine the eggs, heavy cream, salt, black pepper, and ground nutmeg.
5. Combine the ingredients and whisk them together until they are well blended and thoroughly mixed.
6. Evenly distribute the egg mixture over the bacon and cheese in the pie crust, ensuring that it covers the ingredients completely.
7. Put the quiche into the oven that has been preheated and let it bake for approximately 45 to 50 minutes, or until the center is fully set and the top turns a golden brown color.

8. After removing the quiche from the oven, it is recommended to let it cool for a short while before serving to achieve an optimal temperature.
9. If desired, sprinkle chopped fresh chives over the top for added flavor and garnish.
10. Slice the quiche and serve it warm as a delightful breakfast or brunch option for two.

Nutritional breakdown per serving:

Calories: 750-800 kcal, Protein: 28 grams, Carbohydrates: 25 grams, Fat: 60 grams, Saturated Fat: 32 grams, Cholesterol: 370 milligrams, Sodium: 1100 milligrams, Fiber: 1 grams, and Sugar: 2 grams.

WHOLE-GRAIN BREAKFAST BURRITO

- Prep Time: 15 minutes
- Total Cooking Time: 15 minutes
- Servings: 2

Ingredients:

- 4 large eggs
- 1 tablespoon olive oil
- 1/4 cup diced onion
- 1/4 cup diced bell pepper
- 1/4 cup diced tomato
- 1/4 cup shredded cheddar cheese
- 2 whole-grain tortillas
- Salt and pepper to taste

Optional toppings:

- Salsa
- Avocado slices
- Fresh cilantro

Directions:

1. Take a bowl and vigorously whisk the eggs until they are thoroughly beaten. Set the whisked eggs aside for later use.
2. When preparing for cooking, start by placing a skillet on the stove. Following this step, heat the olive oil over medium heat until it reaches the ideal cooking temperature.
3. Once the diced onion and bell pepper are in the skillet, sauté them for 2-3 minutes until the vegetables are slightly softened.
4. Introduce the diced tomato to the skillet and continue cooking for an additional 1-2 minutes.
5. Create a division in the skillet by pushing the vegetables to one side, then pour the beaten eggs into the other side. Season with salt and pepper.
6. Proceed to cook the eggs, stirring occasionally, until they reach your desired consistency.

7. After the eggs are cooked, sprinkle the shredded cheddar cheese on top. Keep stirring until the cheese is fully melted and blends smoothly with the eggs and vegetables.
8. Warm the whole-grain tortillas in a separate skillet or microwave.
9. Divide the scrambled eggs and vegetable mixture between the two tortillas, placing the filling in the center of each tortilla.
10. Wrap the sides of the tortillas over the filling, then roll them tightly to create burritos.
11. Optional: If desired, lightly toast the burritos in a skillet for a few minutes to give them a crispy texture.
12. Serve the whole-grain breakfast burritos warm, with optional toppings such as salsa, avocado slices, and fresh cilantro.

Nutritional breakdown per serving:

Calories: 350-400 kcal, Protein: 20 grams, Carbohydrates: 25 grams, Fat: 20 grams, Saturated Fat: 7 grams, Cholesterol: 390 milligrams, Sodium: 490 milligrams, Fiber: 4 grams, and Sugar: 4 grams.

APPLE CINNAMON OVERNIGHT OATS

- Prep Time: 10 minutes
- Total Cooking Time: Overnight (at least 6-8 hours)
- Servings: 2

Ingredients:

- 1 cup rolled oats
- 1 cup almond milk
- 1/2 cup Greek yogurt
- 1 medium apple, cored and chopped
- 2 tablespoons maple syrup (or honey)
- 1 teaspoon ground cinnamon
- 1/4 teaspoon vanilla extract
- Pinch of salt

Optional toppings:

- Chopped nuts (e.g., walnuts, almonds)
- Dried cranberries or raisins
- Additional sliced apples
- Drizzle of maple syrup

Directions:

1. In a medium-sized bowl, combine the rolled oats, almond milk, Greek yogurt, maple syrup, ground cinnamon, vanilla extract, and salt. Stir well to combine.
2. Include the diced apple in the mixture and stir to ensure even distribution of the apple.
3. Separate the mixture into two jars or containers with lids.
4. Place the lids on the jars or containers and refrigerate them overnight, or for a minimum of 6-8 hours, to give the oats time to soften and absorb the flavors.
5. In the morning, give the overnight oats a good stir.
6. If desired, add optional toppings such as chopped nuts, dried cranberries or raisins, additional sliced apples, and a drizzle of maple syrup.
7. Enjoy the apple cinnamon overnight oats cold or at room temperature.

Nutritional breakdown per serving:

Calories: 300-350 kcal, Protein: 11 grams, Carbohydrates: 55 grams, Fat: 6 grams, Saturated Fat: 1 grams, Cholesterol: 3 milligrams, Sodium: 120 milligrams, Fiber: 8 grams, and Sugar: 22 grams.

VEGGIE BREAKFAST WRAP

- Prep Time: 10 minutes
- Total Cooking Time: 10 minutes
- Servings: 2

Ingredients:

- 4 large eggs
- 2 large whole wheat tortillas
- 1/2 cup diced bell peppers
- 1/2 cup diced tomatoes
- 1/4 cup diced red onions
- 1/4 cup shredded cheddar cheese
- 1/4 teaspoon salt
- 1/4 teaspoon black pepper
- 1 tablespoon olive oil

Optional toppings:

- Sliced avocado
- Salsa
- Fresh cilantro

Directions:

1. Whisk the eggs in a bowl until they are well beaten, and then set them aside.
2. Cook the olive oil in a skillet over medium heat.
3. Add the diced bell peppers, tomatoes, and red onions to the skillet. Sauté for 3-4 minutes until the vegetables are slightly softened.
4. After moving the vegetables to one side of the skillet, pour the beaten eggs onto the other side, and then season with salt and black pepper.
5. Prepare the eggs by stirring occasionally until they are scrambled and fully cooked.
6. Warm the whole wheat tortillas in a separate skillet or microwave.
7. Divide the scrambled eggs and sautéed vegetables between the two tortillas, placing the filling in the center of each tortilla.
8. Sprinkle shredded cheddar cheese over the filling.

9. Optional: Add sliced avocado, salsa, or fresh cilantro as desired.

10. Wrap the sides of the tortillas over the filling, then roll them up tightly to form wraps.

11. Serve the veggie breakfast wraps warm, and enjoy them as a delicious and nutritious breakfast option for two.

Nutritional breakdown per serving:

Calories: 350-400 kcal, Protein: 20 grams, Carbohydrates: 25 grams, Fat: 20 grams, Saturated Fat: 7 grams, Cholesterol: 340 milligrams, Sodium: 600 milligrams, Fiber: 20 grams, and Sugar: 4 grams.

BLUEBERRY PROTEIN PANCAKES

- Prep Time: 10 minutes
- Total Cooking Time: 15 minutes
- Servings: 2 (6 pancakes in total)

Ingredients:

- 1 cup whole wheat flour
- 1 scoop (about 30g) vanilla protein powder
- 1 teaspoon baking powder
- 1/2 teaspoon baking soda
- 1/4 teaspoon salt
- 1 cup unsweetened almond milk
- 1 large egg
- 1 tablespoon honey (or maple syrup)
- 1 teaspoon vanilla extract
- 1/2 cup fresh or frozen blueberries
- Cooking spray or oil for greasing the pan

Optional toppings:

- Additional blueberries
- Greek yogurt
- Maple syrup

Directions:

1. In a large bowl, mix together the whole wheat flour, protein powder, baking powder, baking soda, and salt, then use a whisk to blend the ingredients.
2. Take a separate bowl and mix together the almond milk, egg, honey, and vanilla extract. Thoroughly combine the ingredients by whisking them together until they are well mixed.
3. Carefully combine the wet ingredients with the dry ingredients by pouring them into the bowl and gently stirring until they are just blended together. It's important not to overmix the batter, as it is perfectly fine to have some lumps remaining.

4. Incorporate the blueberries into the pancake batter with care, using a gentle folding motion to ensure they are evenly distributed.

5. Set a non-stick skillet or griddle on the stovetop and heat it over medium heat until it becomes fully preheated. Next, coat the surface with a thin layer of cooking spray or oil to ensure the food doesn't stick while cooking.

6. Use a measuring cup with a 1/4 cup capacity to pour the batter onto the skillet for each pancake. Cook the pancake until bubbles appear on the surface, then gently flip it and cook for an additional 1-2 minutes until it achieves a desirable golden brown color.

7. Continue the process with the remaining batter, applying a thin layer of grease to the skillet as necessary.

8. Serve the warm blueberry protein pancakes and optionally garnish with extra blueberries, a spoonful of Greek yogurt, and a drizzle of maple syrup.

Nutritional breakdown per serving (3 pancakes):
Calories: 350-400 kcal, Protein: 20 grams, Carbohydrates: 55 grams, Fat: 6 grams, Saturated Fat: 1 grams, Cholesterol: 60 milligrams, Sodium: 450 milligrams, Fiber: 8 grams, and Sugar: 13 grams.

BREAKFAST QUINOA SALAD

- Prep Time: 10 minutes
- Total Cooking Time: 20 minutes
- Servings: 2

Ingredients:
- 1/2 cup quinoa
- 1 cup water
- 4 large eggs
- 1 cup baby spinach leaves
- 1/2 cup cherry tomatoes, halved
- 1/4 cup diced cucumber
- 1/4 cup diced red bell pepper
- 2 tablespoons chopped fresh parsley
- 2 tablespoons extra-virgin olive oil
- 1 tablespoon lemon juice
- Salt and pepper to taste

Optional toppings:

- Avocado slices
- Feta cheese crumbles
- Toasted nuts or seeds

Directions:
1. Using a fine-mesh sieve, rinse the quinoa under cold water until it is thoroughly cleansed. Make sure to drain it well before moving forward.
2. Simmer the quinoa over low heat, covered, for approximately 15 minutes until it becomes tender and absorbs the water.
3. Afterward, take the saucepan off the heat, cover it, and allow it to rest for an extra 5 minutes.
4. While the quinoa is cooking, place the eggs in a separate saucepan and cover them with water. Bring to a boil over high heat.

5. Once boiling, reduce the heat to low and simmer the eggs for 8-10 minutes for hard-boiled eggs or 4-5 minutes for soft-boiled eggs.

6. After draining the eggs, rinse them under cold water and proceed to peel and slice them.

7. In a large bowl, combine the cooked quinoa, baby spinach leaves, cherry tomatoes, diced cucumber, diced red bell pepper, and chopped fresh parsley.

8. Create the dressing by combining the olive oil, lemon juice, salt, and pepper in a small bowl. Whisk the ingredients together until they are fully blended.

9. Coat the quinoa salad by pouring the dressing over it and tossing until it is thoroughly coated.

10. Place the salad onto two plates or bowls, dividing it evenly. Add the sliced boiled eggs on top as a topping.

11. Optional: Add toppings such as avocado slices, feta cheese crumbles, or toasted nuts or seeds.

12. Serve the breakfast quinoa salad immediately, and enjoy it as a nutritious and flavorful way to start your day.

Nutritional breakdown per serving:

Calories: 350-400 kcal, Protein: 15 grams, Carbohydrates: 30 grams, Fat: 20 grams, Saturated Fat: 4 grams, Cholesterol: 340 milligrams, Sodium: 180 milligrams, Fiber: 6 grams, and Sugar: 3 grams.

EGG AND VEGGIE MUFFINS

- Prep Time: 15 minutes
- Total Cooking Time: 25 minutes
- Servings: 2 (6 muffins in total)

Ingredients:
- 6 large eggs
- 1/4 cup diced bell peppers
- 1/4 cup diced onions
- 1/4 cup diced tomatoes
- 1/4 cup chopped spinach
- 1/4 cup shredded cheddar cheese
- 1/2 teaspoon dried oregano
- 1/4 teaspoon salt
- 1/4 teaspoon black pepper
- Apply cooking spray or oil to coat the muffin tin

Directions:
1. Prior to starting, ensure that your oven is preheated to 350°F (175°C). Then, coat a 6-cup muffin tin with cooking spray or oil to prevent sticking.
2. Take a bowl and whisk the eggs vigorously until they are thoroughly beaten and well combined.
3. Add the diced bell peppers, onions, tomatoes, chopped spinach, shredded cheddar cheese, dried oregano, salt, and black pepper to the beaten eggs. Stir well to combine.
4. Ensure an equal distribution of the egg and veggie mixture among the greased muffin cups, filling each cup approximately 3/4 full.
5. Once you have placed the muffin tray in the preheated oven, allow the muffins to bake for approximately 20-25 minutes until they are cooked through and develop a delightful light golden color on the surface.
6. Once you have taken the muffin tin out of the oven, it is important to allow the muffins to cool for a few minutes before handling them.
7. Gently take the muffins out of the tin and serve them while still warm.

Nutritional breakdown per serving (3 muffins):

Calories: 250-300 kcal, Protein: 22 grams, Carbohydrates: 5 grams, Fat: 15 grams, Saturated Fat: 6 grams, Cholesterol: 420 milligrams, Sodium: 450 milligrams, Fiber: 1 grams, and Sugar: 2 grams.

ALMOND BUTTER BANANA SMOOTHIE

- Prep Time: 5 minutes
- Total Cooking Time: 5 minutes
- Servings: 2

Ingredients:

- 2 ripe bananas, peeled and sliced
- 2 tablespoons almond butter
- 1 cup unsweetened almond milk
- 1 cup ice cubes
- 1 tablespoon honey
- 1/2 teaspoon vanilla extract

Optional toppings:

- Sliced bananas
- Crushed almonds
- Drizzle of honey

Directions:

1. Place the sliced bananas, almond butter, almond milk, ice cubes, honey (if using), and vanilla extract in a blender.
2. Using a high-speed blender, blend the ingredients until they are thoroughly combined and the smoothie achieves a creamy and smooth consistency.
3. After taking a moment to appreciate the smoothie, experience its taste by sampling it. If you wish for a sweeter flavor, customize the sweetness to your preference by incorporating additional honey.
4. Pour the smoothie into two glasses.
5. Optional: Top the smoothies with sliced bananas, crushed almonds, and a drizzle of honey for added texture and presentation.
6. Serve the almond butter banana smoothies immediately, and enjoy them as a refreshing and nutritious treat for two.

Nutritional breakdown per serving:

Calories: 250-300 kcal, Protein: 6 grams, Carbohydrates: 35 grams, Fat: 12 grams, Saturated Fat: 1 grams, Cholesterol: 0 milligrams, Sodium: 160 milligrams, Fiber: 6 grams, and Sugar: 17 grams.

MEDITERRANEAN EGG SCRAMBLE

- Prep Time: 10 minutes
- Total Cooking Time: 15 minutes
- Servings: 2

Ingredients:
- 4 large eggs
- 1 tablespoon olive oil
- 1/4 cup diced red onion
- 1/2 cup diced bell peppers
- 1/2 cup diced tomatoes
- 1/4 cup sliced black olives
- 1/4 cup crumbled feta cheese
- 1/4 teaspoon dried oregano
- Salt and pepper to taste
- Fresh chopped parsley for garnish (optional)

Directions:
1. Whisk the eggs thoroughly in a bowl until they are well beaten, and then set the bowl aside for further use.
2. Carefully warm the olive oil in a non-stick skillet over a medium heat setting.
3. Add the diced red onion and bell peppers to the skillet. Sauté for 2-3 minutes until slightly softened.
4. Add the diced tomatoes and sliced black olives to the skillet. Cook for another 2 minutes, stirring occasionally.
5. Reduce the heat to low and pour the beaten eggs into the skillet. Stir gently to combine the eggs with the vegetables.
6. Sprinkle the crumbled feta cheese and dried oregano over the egg mixture. Season with salt and pepper to taste.
7. While cooking the egg mixture, stir it occasionally until the eggs reach a fully cooked consistency that is moist and slightly creamy.
8. Take the skillet off the heat and carefully transfer the Mediterranean egg scramble onto serving plates.

9. For an optional touch, you can enhance the freshness and presentation by garnishing the dish with freshly chopped parsley.
10. Serve the Mediterranean egg scramble immediately, and enjoy it as a flavorful and satisfying breakfast or brunch for two.

Nutritional breakdown per serving:

Calories: 250-300 kcal, Protein: 15 grams, Carbohydrates: 8 grams, Fat: 18 grams, Saturated Fat: 6 grams, Cholesterol: 370 milligrams, Sodium: 400 milligrams, Fiber: 2 grams, and Sugar: 4 grams.

CHAPTER 2
LUNCH

GRILLED CHICKEN SALAD

- Prep Time: 15 minutes
- Total Cooking Time: 20 minutes
- Servings: 2

Ingredients:

- 2 boneless, skinless chicken breasts
- 4 cups mixed salad greens
- 1 cup cherry tomatoes, halved
- 1/2 cup sliced cucumber
- 1/4 cup sliced red onion
- 1/4 cup sliced black olives
- 1/4 cup crumbled feta cheese
- 2 tablespoons chopped fresh parsley
- 2 tablespoons extra-virgin olive oil
- 1 tablespoon lemon juice
- 1 clove garlic, minced
- Salt and pepper to taste

Directions:

1. Before you begin, preheat a grill or grill pan over medium heat.
2. Customize the seasoning of the chicken breasts by adding salt and pepper to suit your personal taste preferences.
3. Once you have confirmed that the grill is preheated, carefully position the chicken breasts on the grill grates and allow them to cook for approximately 6-8 minutes on each side. Cook the chicken until it is fully done and the center is no longer pink in color.
4. Take the grilled chicken off the grill and allow it to rest for a few minutes. Afterward, proceed to slice it into thin strips.
5. In a spacious bowl, mix together the assorted salad greens, cherry tomatoes, sliced cucumber, sliced red onion, sliced black olives, crumbled feta cheese, and freshly chopped parsley.
6. In a small bowl, whisk together the extra-virgin olive oil, lemon juice, minced garlic, salt, and pepper to make the dressing.

7. Drizzle the dressing evenly over the salad mixture and toss thoroughly to ensure that all the ingredients are coated with the dressing.
8. Distribute the salad mixture equally among two plates or bowls.
9. Top each salad with the sliced grilled chicken.
10. Optional: Garnish with additional parsley if desired.
11. Serve the grilled chicken salad immediately, and enjoy it as a delicious and nutritious meal for two.

Nutritional breakdown per serving:
Calories: 350-400 kcal, Protein: 35 grams, Carbohydrates: 10 grams, Fat: 20 grams, Saturated Fat: 5 grams, Cholesterol: 80 milligrams, Sodium: 400 milligrams, Fiber: 3 grams, and Sugar: 4 grams.

QUINOA STUFFED BELL PEPPERS

- Prep Time: 20 minutes
- Total Cooking Time: 45 minutes
- Servings: 2 (2 stuffed bell peppers)

Ingredients:

- 2 large bell peppers (any color)
- 1/2 cup uncooked quinoa
- 1 cup vegetable broth or water
- 1 tablespoon olive oil
- 1/4 cup diced onion
- 1/4 cup diced zucchini
- 1/4 cup diced red bell pepper
- 1/4 cup diced yellow bell pepper
- 1/2 cup of canned black beans, after rinsing and draining
- 1/2 cup canned diced tomatoes
- 1/2 teaspoon ground cumin
- 1/2 teaspoon paprika
- Salt and pepper to taste
- 1/4 cup shredded cheddar cheese (optional)
- Fresh cilantro or parsley for garnish (optional)

Directions:

1. To achieve the desired temperature of 375°F (190°C), preheat the oven and allow it to reach the designated temperature while exercising patience.
2. Start by cutting off the tops of the bell peppers, then proceed to remove the seeds and membranes. Set them aside for later use.
3. In a fine-mesh sieve, rinse the quinoa under cold water. Drain well.
4. Using a medium-sized saucepan, bring either vegetable broth or water to a boil. Add the rinsed quinoa to the pan, then lower the heat to a simmer and cover it. Allow the quinoa to cook for approximately 15 minutes, or until it is fully cooked and has absorbed the liquid. After the quinoa is fully cooked, take the pan off the heat and gently fluff the quinoa using a fork.

5. As the quinoa continues to cook, prepare a skillet by heating the olive oil over medium heat.

6. Add the diced onion, zucchini, red bell pepper, and yellow bell pepper to the skillet. Sauté for 5-6 minutes until the vegetables are tender.

7. In the heated skillet, incorporate the canned black beans, diced tomatoes, ground cumin, paprika, salt, and pepper. Stir well to combine and cook for another 2-3 minutes.

8. Take the skillet off the heat and combine the cooked quinoa with the vegetable mixture. Carefully combine all the ingredients, ensuring they are thoroughly mixed and evenly distributed throughout.

9. Take the quinoa and vegetable mixture and tightly pack it into the bell peppers, effectively stuffing them.

10. Position the stuffed bell peppers in an upright position within a baking dish. For added flavor, you have the option to generously sprinkle shredded cheddar cheese over the top of each stuffed pepper.

11. After covering the baking dish with foil, place it in the preheated oven and bake for approximately 25 minutes.

12. Take off the foil covering and place the baking dish back into the oven for another 5-10 minutes. Bake until the bell peppers become tender, and the cheese is fully melted and forms a delicious bubbly crust.

13. Once done baking, take the stuffed bell peppers out of the oven and allow them to cool for a few minutes before serving.

14. For an optional touch, you can enhance the presentation by adding a garnish of fresh cilantro or parsley before serving.

15. Present the quinoa stuffed bell peppers as a satisfying and nourishing meal, perfect for two individuals to enjoy.

Nutritional breakdown per serving (1 stuffed bell pepper):
Calories: 300-350 kcal, Protein: 12 grams, Carbohydrates: 45 grams, Fat: 10 grams, Saturated Fat: 3 grams, Cholesterol: 10 milligrams, Sodium: 550 milligrams, Fiber: 10 grams, and Sugar: 10 grams.

SALMON AND ASPARAGUS FOIL PACKETS

- Prep Time: 15 minutes
- Total Cooking Time: 20 minutes
- Servings: 2

Ingredients:

- 2 salmon fillets (6-8 ounces each)
- 1 bunch asparagus, tough ends trimmed
- 2 tablespoons olive oil
- 2 cloves garlic, minced
- 1 lemon, sliced
- Salt and pepper to taste
- Fresh dill or parsley for garnish (optional)

Directions:

1. To start, adjust the oven to a temperature of 425°F (220°C).
2. Cut two large sheets of aluminum foil, approximately 12x18 inches each.
3. Position a single salmon fillet in the middle of every foil sheet.
4. Divide the asparagus evenly and arrange it around the salmon fillets.
5. In a compact bowl, combine the olive oil, minced garlic, salt, and pepper, whisking diligently until they are completely mixed together.
6. Carefully pour the olive oil mixture over both the salmon and asparagus, ensuring they are thoroughly coated.
7. Arrange several slices of lemon on the surface of each salmon fillet.
8. Take the edges of the foil and fold them securely over the salmon and asparagus, creating a tightly sealed packet.
9. Carefully position the foil packets on a baking sheet, ensuring they are evenly spread out with the right amount of spacing. Proceed to carefully insert the baking sheet into the preheated oven, exercising caution.
10. Allow the contents to bake for a duration of 15 to 18 minutes, or until the salmon is thoroughly cooked and can be easily separated into flakes using a fork.
11. Gently unfold the foil packets, taking care to be mindful of the hot steam.
12. Optional: Garnish with fresh dill or parsley for added flavor and presentation.

13. Serve the salmon and asparagus foil packets immediately, allowing each person to enjoy their own delicious and nutritious meal.

Nutritional breakdown per serving:
Calories: 350-400 kcal, Protein: 30 grams, Carbohydrates: 7 grams, Fat: 25 grams, Saturated Fat: 4 grams, Cholesterol: 80 milligrams, Sodium: 100 milligrams, Fiber: 3 grams, and Sugar: 2 grams.

GREEK SALAD WITH GRILLED SHRIMP

- Prep Time: 20 minutes
- Total Cooking Time: 10 minutes
- Servings: 2

Ingredients:
For the Greek Salad:

- 4 cups mixed salad greens
- 1 cup cherry tomatoes, halved
- 1/2 cup sliced cucumber
- 1/4 cup sliced red onion
- 1/4 cup sliced Kalamata olives
- 1/4 cup crumbled feta cheese
- 2 tablespoons chopped fresh parsley
- 2 tablespoons extra-virgin olive oil
- 1 tablespoon red wine vinegar
- Salt and pepper to taste

For the Grilled Shrimp:

- 12 large shrimp, peeled and deveined
- 1 tablespoon olive oil
- 2 cloves garlic, minced
- 1/2 teaspoon dried oregano
- Salt and pepper to taste
- Lemon wedges for serving (optional)

Directions:
1. Before utilizing, heat a grill or grill pan over medium-high heat until it reaches the preferred temperature.
2. Combine the mixed salad greens, cherry tomatoes, cucumber slices, red onion slices, Kalamata olives, crumbled feta cheese, and freshly chopped parsley in a large bowl.

3. In a small bowl, whisk together the extra-virgin olive oil, red wine vinegar, salt, and pepper to make the dressing for the Greek salad. Set aside.
4. In a separate bowl, combine the olive oil, minced garlic, dried oregano, salt, and pepper. Place the peeled and deveined shrimp into the bowl, and toss them gently until they are fully coated with the marinade.
5. Thread the marinated shrimp onto skewers, if using, or place them directly on the preheated grill or grill pan.
6. Cook the shrimp for 2-3 minutes per side, or until they are pink and opaque.
7. As the shrimp grill, distribute the dressing evenly over the salad mixture and delicately toss it to guarantee that all the ingredients are coated with the dressing.
8. Divide the Greek salad between two plates or bowls.
9. Once the shrimp are cooked, remove them from the grill and place them on top of the Greek salad.
10. Optional: Squeeze fresh lemon juice over the grilled shrimp before serving for added zest.
11. Promptly serve the Greek salad with grilled shrimp and relish it as a revitalizing and gratifying meal designed for two.

Nutritional breakdown per serving:
Calories: 300-350 kcal, Protein: 25 grams, Carbohydrates: 15 grams, Fat: 20 grams, Saturated Fat: 5 grams, Cholesterol: 160 milligrams, Sodium: 600 milligrams, Fiber: 4 grams, and Sugar: 5 grams.

LENTIL VEGETABLE SOUP

- Prep Time: 15 minutes
- Total Cooking Time: 45 minutes
- Servings: 2

Ingredients:

- 1 tablespoon olive oil
- 1/2 cup diced onion
- 1/2 cup diced carrot
- 1/2 cup diced celery
- 2 cloves garlic, minced
- 1/2 cup dried lentils (any variety), rinsed and drained
- 3 cups vegetable broth
- 1 cup diced tomatoes (canned or fresh)
- 1 bay leaf
- 1 teaspoon dried thyme
- 1/2 teaspoon ground cumin
- 1/2 teaspoon paprika
- Salt and pepper to taste
- 2 cups chopped mixed vegetables (such as zucchini, bell peppers, and spinach)
- Fresh parsley for garnish (optional)

Directions:

1. Place the large pot over medium heat and heat the olive oil until it reaches a warmed temperature.
2. Add the diced onion, carrot, and celery to the pot. Sauté for 5 minutes until the vegetables start to soften.
3. Add the minced garlic and sauté for an additional minute.
4. Add the rinsed lentils, vegetable broth, diced tomatoes, bay leaf, dried thyme, ground cumin, paprika, salt, and pepper to the pot. Stir well to combine.
5. Achieve a boiling point for the soup and subsequently lower the heat to a low setting. Proceed by covering the pot with a lid and allowing the soup to simmer for

approximately 30 minutes, or until the lentils have softened to the desired level of tenderness.

6. At the 30-minute mark, introduce the chopped mixed vegetables into the pot. Stir the contents thoroughly and continue cooking for an additional 10 minutes, or until the vegetables have reached the desired level of tenderness.
7. Remove the bay leaf from the soup.
8. Sample the soup and, if necessary, make adjustments to the seasoning by adding salt and pepper to achieve the desired taste.
9. Ladle the lentil vegetable soup into bowls.
10. Optional: Garnish with fresh parsley for added flavor and presentation.
11. Serve the lentil vegetable soup hot, and enjoy it as a comforting and nutritious meal for two.

Nutritional breakdown per serving:

Calories: 250-300 kcal, Protein: 15 grams, Carbohydrates: 40 grams, Fat: 6 grams, Saturated Fat: 1 grams, Cholesterol: 0 milligrams, Sodium: 800 milligrams, Fiber: 15 grams, and Sugar: 8 grams.

TURKEY LETTUCE WRAPS

- Prep Time: 15 minutes
- Total Cooking Time: 15 minutes
- Servings: 2

Ingredients:

- 1 tablespoon olive oil
- 1/2 cup diced onion
- 1/2 cup diced bell pepper (any color)
- 1/2 cup shredded carrots
- 2 cloves garlic, minced
- 1/2 pound ground turkey
- 2 tablespoons soy sauce
- 1 tablespoon hoisin sauce
- 1 tablespoon rice vinegar
- 1 teaspoon sesame oil
- 1 teaspoon grated fresh ginger
- Salt and pepper to taste
- 1 head of lettuce (such as Bibb or iceberg), leaves separated
- Optional toppings: chopped green onions, chopped peanuts, sriracha sauce

Directions:

1. Prepare the stovetop by placing a large skillet or wok over medium-high heat, and proceed to heat the olive oil until it reaches the desired temperature.
2. Add the diced onion, bell pepper, and shredded carrots to the skillet. Sauté for 3-4 minutes until the vegetables start to soften.
3. Incorporate the minced garlic into the skillet, ensuring it comes into contact with the heat, and sauté it for an additional minute.
4. With the vegetables pushed to one side of the skillet, proceed to add the ground turkey to the opposite side. Utilize a spatula to break up the turkey as it cooks, ensuring it turns brown and reaches a fully cooked state.
5. In a small bowl, whisk together the soy sauce, hoisin sauce, rice vinegar, sesame oil, grated ginger, salt, and pepper.

6. Ensure that all the ingredients in the skillet, including the cooked turkey and vegetables, are covered by pouring the sauce over them. Cook for an additional 2-3 minutes until the flavors are well combined.
7. Remove the skillet from the heat.
8. Scoop the turkey mixture onto the lettuce leaves using a spoon, making sure to distribute it evenly among the leaves.
9. Optional: Top the lettuce wraps with chopped green onions, chopped peanuts, and/or a drizzle of sriracha sauce for added flavor and crunch.
10. Serve the turkey lettuce wraps immediately, allowing each person to wrap the filling in the lettuce leaves and enjoy a delicious and healthy meal for two.

Nutritional breakdown per serving:
Calories: 280-320 kcal, Protein: 22 grams, Carbohydrates: 16 grams, Fat: 16 grams, Saturated Fat: 3 grams, Cholesterol: 60 milligrams, Sodium: 800 milligrams, Fiber: 4 grams, and Sugar: 6 grams.

QUINOA AND BLACK BEAN SALAD

- Prep Time: 15 minutes
- Total Cooking Time: 20 minutes (plus cooling time for quinoa)
- Servings: 2

Ingredients:
- 1/2 cup quinoa
- 1 cup vegetable broth or water
- 1 cup of canned black beans, having been rinsed and drained
- 1/2 cup diced red bell pepper
- 1/2 cup diced cucumber
- 1/4 cup chopped red onion
- 1/4 cup chopped fresh cilantro
- 2 tablespoons lime juice
- 1 tablespoon extra-virgin olive oil
- 1 clove garlic, minced
- 1/2 teaspoon ground cumin
- Salt and pepper to taste
- Optional toppings: avocado slices, cherry tomatoes, crumbled feta cheese

Directions:
1. To eliminate any bitter taste, rinse the quinoa thoroughly under cold water, making use of a fine-mesh sieve.
2. Using a small saucepan, bring the vegetable broth or water to a boil. After that, add the rinsed quinoa to the saucepan and lower the heat to a low setting. Maintain the saucepan covered and allow the quinoa to simmer for roughly 15 minutes, or until it becomes tender and completely absorbs all the liquid.
3. Take the cooked quinoa off the heat and allow it to cool for a few minutes.
4. In a large bowl, combine the cooked quinoa, black beans, diced red bell pepper, diced cucumber, chopped red onion, and chopped cilantro.
5. In a separate small bowl, whisk together the lime juice, extra-virgin olive oil, minced garlic, ground cumin, salt, and pepper.
6. Drizzle the dressing over the mixture of quinoa and black beans, ensuring that all the ingredients are evenly coated. Toss gently to distribute the dressing.

7. Let the salad sit for at least 10 minutes to allow the flavors to meld together.
8. Optional: Before serving, top the salad with avocado slices, cherry tomatoes, and crumbled feta cheese for added flavor and texture.
9. You can serve the quinoa and black bean salad either at room temperature or chilled. It's a nutritious and satisfying meal that is perfect for two people to enjoy.

Nutritional breakdown per serving:
Calories: 350-400 kcal, Protein: 14 grams, Carbohydrates: 55 grams, Fat: 12 grams, Saturated Fat: 2 grams, Cholesterol: 0 milligrams, Sodium: 400 milligrams, Fiber: 14 grams, and Sugar: 5 grams.

GRILLED VEGETABLE WRAP

- Prep Time: 20 minutes
- Total Cooking Time: 15 minutes
- Servings: 2

Ingredients:

- 2 large flour tortillas
- 1 medium zucchini, sliced lengthwise
- 1 medium yellow squash, sliced lengthwise
- 1 red bell pepper, seeded and quartered
- 1 small red onion, sliced into rounds
- 2 tablespoons olive oil
- Salt and pepper to taste
- 4 tablespoons hummus
- 1 cup fresh spinach leaves
- Optional toppings: sliced avocado, crumbled feta cheese, fresh herbs (such as basil or cilantro)

Directions:

1. Preheat the grill to medium-high heat.
2. Brush the zucchini, yellow squash, red bell pepper, and red onion slices with olive oil. Season with salt and pepper.
3. Position the vegetables on the grill and grill each side for approximately 4-5 minutes, or until they reach a tender texture and acquire a desirable charred appearance.
4. Remove the grilled vegetables from the heat and let them cool slightly.
5. Take the grilled vegetables off the heat and allow them to cool slightly. Meanwhile, heat the flour tortillas on the grill for about a minute on each side, or until they become flexible and warm.
6. Take 2 tablespoons of hummus and spread it evenly onto each tortilla, ensuring to leave a small border around the edges.
7. Layer the grilled vegetables and fresh spinach leaves on top of the hummus.
8. Optional: Add sliced avocado, crumbled feta cheese, or fresh herbs as desired.
9. Roll up the tortillas tightly, tucking in the sides as you go.
10. Slice the wraps in half diagonally, if desired, for easier handling.

11. Serve the grilled vegetable wraps immediately or wrap them in foil for later enjoyment.
12. Enjoy these delicious and wholesome grilled vegetable wraps as a satisfying meal for two.

Nutritional breakdown per serving:
Calories: 400-450 kcal, Protein: 10 grams, Carbohydrates: 44 grams, Fat: 22 grams, Saturated Fat: 4 grams, Cholesterol: 0 milligrams, Sodium: 600 milligrams, Fiber: 8 grams, and Sugar: 6 grams.

SHRIMP AND BROCCOLI STIR-FRY

- Prep Time: 15 minutes
- Total Cooking Time: 15 minutes
- Servings: 2

Ingredients:

- 1/2 pound shrimp, peeled and deveined
- 2 cups broccoli florets
- 1 medium carrot, sliced
- 1/2 red bell pepper, sliced
- 2 cloves garlic, minced
- 1 tablespoon grated fresh ginger
- 2 tablespoons soy sauce
- 1 tablespoon oyster sauce
- 1 tablespoon rice vinegar
- 1 teaspoon cornstarch
- 1 tablespoon vegetable oil (for cooking)
- Salt and pepper to taste
- Optional toppings: sliced green onions, sesame seeds

Directions:

1. Combine the soy sauce, oyster sauce, rice vinegar, cornstarch, and a pinch of salt and pepper in a small bowl. Blend the ingredients thoroughly by whisking them together, and then set the mixture aside for later use.
2. Heat up the vegetable oil in a spacious skillet or wok over medium-high heat.
3. Introduce the minced garlic and grated ginger into the skillet and sauté them for approximately 1 minute until they release a fragrant aroma.
4. Position the shrimp in the skillet and proceed to cook them for approximately 2-3 minutes, or until they transform into a pink color and achieve an opaque appearance. Once done, remove the shrimp from the skillet and set them aside for later use.

5. Using the same skillet, introduce the broccoli florets, carrot slices, and red bell pepper slices. Stir-fry the vegetables for about 4-5 minutes until they reach a crisp-tender texture.
6. Return the shrimp to the skillet with the vegetables.
7. Drizzle the sauce mixture over the shrimp and vegetables in the skillet, ensuring that all ingredients are evenly coated. Stir thoroughly to distribute the sauce evenly across everything.
8. Extend the cooking time by 1-2 minutes to allow the sauce to thicken and evenly coat both the shrimp and vegetables.
9. Remove the skillet from the heat.
10. Consider enhancing the stir-fry by adding sliced green onions and sesame seeds for an extra boost of flavor and texture.
11. To savor a delectable and wholesome meal for two, present the shrimp and broccoli stir-fry over a bed of steamed rice or noodles.

Nutritional breakdown per serving:
Calories: 140-300 kcal, Protein: 25 grams, Carbohydrates: 15 grams, Fat: 10 grams, Saturated Fat: 1.5 grams, Cholesterol: 120 milligrams, Sodium: 1000 milligrams, Fiber: 4 grams, and Sugar: 6 grams.

CHICKPEA SALAD

- Prep Time: 15 minutes
- Total Cooking Time: 0 minutes (no cooking required)
- Servings: 2

Ingredients:

- 2 cups canned chickpeas, rinsed and drained
- 1 cup cherry tomatoes, halved
- 1 cucumber, diced
- 1/4 cup red onion, finely chopped
- 1/4 cup chopped fresh parsley
- 2 tablespoons extra-virgin olive oil
- 2 tablespoons lemon juice
- 1 clove garlic, minced
- 1/2 teaspoon ground cumin
- Salt and pepper to taste
- Optional toppings: crumbled feta cheese, sliced olives, diced avocado

Directions:

1. In a large bowl, combine the chickpeas, cherry tomatoes, diced cucumber, chopped red onion, and chopped parsley.
2. In a small bowl, whisk together the extra-virgin olive oil, lemon juice, minced garlic, ground cumin, salt, and pepper.
3. Pour the dressing over the chickpea mixture in the large bowl. Carefully toss the ingredients to ensure an even coating.
4. For optimal flavor integration, consider letting the salad rest for around 10 minutes to allow the flavors to meld seamlessly.
5. Optional: Top the chickpea salad with crumbled feta cheese, sliced olives, or diced avocado for added flavor and texture.
6. Serve the chickpea salad as a refreshing and nutritious meal for two.

Nutritional breakdown per serving:
Calories: 300-350 kcal, Protein: 11 grams, Carbohydrates: 38 grams, Fat: 14 grams, Saturated Fat: 2 grams, Cholesterol: 0 milligrams, Sodium: 300 milligrams, Fiber: 10 grams, and Sugar: 6 grams.

SPINACH AND FETA STUFFED CHICKEN BREAST

- Prep Time: 20 minutes
- Total Cooking Time: 35 minutes
- Servings: 2

Ingredients:

- 2 boneless, skinless chicken breasts
- 1 cup fresh spinach leaves
- 1/2 cup crumbled feta cheese
- 1/4 cup chopped sun-dried tomatoes (optional)
- 1 clove garlic, minced
- 1 tablespoon olive oil
- 1/2 teaspoon dried oregano
- Salt and pepper to taste
- Toothpicks or kitchen twine (for securing the stuffed chicken)
- Grease pan (spray or oil)

Directions:

1. To ensure ideal cooking conditions, start by preheating the oven to 375°F (190°C).
2. Create a butterfly effect by making a horizontal cut through the thickest part of each chicken breast, ensuring not to cut all the way through. Then, open the chicken breasts as you would open a book.
3. In a medium-sized bowl, combine the fresh spinach leaves, crumbled feta cheese, chopped sun-dried tomatoes (if using), minced garlic, olive oil, dried oregano, salt, and pepper. Mix well.
4. Divide the spinach and feta mixture evenly, placing it on one side of each butterflied chicken breast.
5. Gently fold the opposite side of the chicken breast over the filling to enclose it securely. If necessary, secure the stuffed chicken breast with toothpicks or kitchen twine to ensure it stays intact during cooking.
6. Thoroughly coat the baking dish with cooking spray or a light drizzle of olive oil to prevent any sticking during cooking.
7. Position the stuffed chicken breasts in the baking dish, ensuring that it has been coated with grease.

8. Season the chicken breasts by sprinkling salt, pepper, and dried oregano on top.

9. Give the chicken a 25-30 minute bake in the preheated oven. Aim for a delicious golden brown and crispy exterior. Remember to check for doneness! For perfectly cooked chicken that won't cause any foodborne illness, make sure the internal temperature reaches 165°F (74°C).

10. Before serving, it is important to let the chicken rest for a short period after taking the baking dish out of the oven.

11. To prepare for serving, remove the toothpicks or twine from the chicken breasts.

12. Enjoy a complete and balanced meal! This flavorful spinach and feta stuffed chicken breast is perfect for two. Complement it with roasted vegetables for added vitamins, or a light salad for a refreshing touch.

Nutritional breakdown per serving:

Calories: 300-350 kcal, Protein: 40 grams, Carbohydrates: 5 grams, Fat: 14 grams, Saturated Fat: 6 grams, Cholesterol: 100 milligrams, Sodium: 500 milligrams, Fiber: 1 grams, and Sugar: 2 grams.

CAPRESE SALAD

- Prep Time: 10 minutes
- Total Cooking Time: 0 minutes (no cooking required)
- Servings: 2

Ingredients:
- 2 large ripe tomatoes
- 8 ounces fresh mozzarella cheese
- 1/4 cup fresh basil leaves
- 2 tablespoons extra-virgin olive oil
- 1 tablespoon balsamic vinegar
- Salt and pepper to taste

Directions:
1. Prepare the tomatoes and mozzarella by slicing them both into even pieces, about ¼-inch thick.
2. For an elegant touch, simply alternate tomato and mozzarella slices in a circle on your serving plate.
3. Nestle fresh basil leaves in between the layers of tomato and mozzarella.
4. Infuse your Caprese with a touch of fresh flavor by adding basil leaves between the tomato and mozzarella slices.
5. Season with salt and pepper to taste.
6. Take a quick pause! Letting the salad rest for a few minutes allows the flavors to meld beautifully for an even tastier experience.
7. Serve the Caprese salad as a light and refreshing appetizer or side dish for two.

Nutritional breakdown per serving:
Calories: 300-350 kcal, Protein: 15 grams, Carbohydrates: 7 grams, Fat: 25 grams, Saturated Fat: 12 grams, Cholesterol: 60 milligrams, Sodium: 400 milligrams, Fiber: 1 grams, and Sugar: 4 grams.

VEGGIE WRAP WITH HUMMUS

- Prep Time: 15 minutes
- Total Cooking Time: 0 minutes (no cooking required)
- Servings: 2

Ingredients:
- 2 large whole wheat tortillas or wraps
- 1/2 cup hummus
- 1/2 cup thinly sliced cucumber
- 1/2 cup thinly sliced bell peppers
- 1/2 cup thinly sliced carrots
- 1/2 cup baby spinach leaves
- 1/4 cup sliced red onion
- Salt and pepper to taste

Directions:
1. Lay out the tortillas or wraps on a clean surface.
2. Spread a generous amount of hummus evenly on each tortilla.
3. Layer the cucumber slices, bell peppers, carrots, baby spinach leaves, and red onion slices on top of the hummus.
4. Season with salt and pepper to taste.
5. To create a secure and delicious wrap, tightly roll each tortilla, tucking the sides inwards as you go.
6. Slice the wraps in half diagonally.
7. Serve the veggie wraps as a delicious and nutritious meal for two.

Nutritional breakdown per serving:
Calories: 250-300 kcal, Protein: 10 grams, Carbohydrates: 35 grams, Fat: 10 grams, Saturated Fat: 1.5 grams, Cholesterol: 0 milligrams, Sodium: 400 milligrams, Fiber: 9 grams, and Sugar: 4 grams.

TUNA SALAD LETTUCE CUPS

- Prep Time: 15 minutes
- Total Cooking Time: 0 minutes (no cooking required)
- Servings: 2

Ingredients:

- 1 can (5 ounces) tuna, drained
- 1/4 cup mayonnaise
- 2 tablespoons diced red onion
- 2 tablespoons diced celery
- 1 tablespoon chopped fresh parsley
- 1 tablespoon lemon juice
- Salt and pepper to taste
- 4 large lettuce leaves (such as iceberg or romaine)
- Optional toppings: sliced cherry tomatoes, sliced cucumbers, avocado slices

Directions:

1. In a medium-sized bowl, flake the drained tuna using a fork.
2. Add the mayonnaise, diced red onion, diced celery, chopped parsley, and lemon juice to the bowl with the tuna.
3. Mix well to combine all the ingredients.
4. Start by building a flavor base with salt and pepper. Taste your tuna salad as you go, adjusting the seasonings until it hits the spot for you.
5. Place a spoonful of the tuna salad mixture onto each lettuce leaf, spreading it evenly along the center.
6. Optional: Top the tuna salad with sliced cherry tomatoes, sliced cucumbers, or avocado slices for added flavor and texture.
7. Fold the sides of each lettuce leaf inward, then roll it up to create a lettuce cup.
8. Assemble the rest of your wraps! Use the remaining lettuce leaves and tuna salad to fill out the tortillas.
9. Serve the tuna salad lettuce cups as a light and satisfying meal for two.

Nutritional breakdown per serving:
Calories: 200-250 kcal, Protein: 15 grams, Carbohydrates: 5 grams, Fat: 15 grams, Saturated Fat: 2 grams, Cholesterol: 20 milligrams, Sodium: 400 milligrams, Fiber: 1 grams, and Sugar: 2 grams.

MEDITERRANEAN QUINOA BOWL

- Prep Time: 15 minutes
- Total Cooking Time: 20 minutes
- Servings: 2

Ingredients:

- 1 cup quinoa
- 2 cups vegetable broth or water
- 1 cup cherry tomatoes, halved
- 1/2 English cucumber, diced
- 1/4 cup pitted kalamata olives, sliced
- 1/4 cup crumbled feta cheese
- 2 tablespoons chopped red onion
- 2 tablespoons chopped fresh parsley
- 2 tablespoons extra-virgin olive oil
- 1 tablespoon lemon juice
- 1 clove garlic, minced
- Salt and pepper to taste
- Optional toppings: sliced avocado, hummus, grilled chicken or shrimp

Directions:

1. Give your quinoa a good rinse under cold running water in a fine-mesh sieve. This removes any bitter coating from the grains.
2. In a saucepan, bring your chosen liquid (vegetable broth or water) to a boil. Simmer it low and slow! Add the rinsed quinoa, reduce heat, cover, and simmer for 15 minutes (or until tender and the liquid disappears).
3. Take the quinoa off the heat and let it sit for a few minutes, covered. This allows the grains to steam and fluff up for a perfect texture.
4. In a large bowl, create a symphony of textures and flavors. Start with the cooked quinoa, then add chopped red onion for a bit of bite, diced cucumber for coolness, sliced kalamata olives for a salty touch, crumbled feta cheese for creaminess, and fresh parsley for a touch of herb. Don't forget the vibrant cherry tomatoes!

5. In a small bowl, whisk together extra-virgin olive oil, tangy lemon juice, pungent minced garlic, a hint of salt, and a sprinkle of freshly cracked pepper. This combination creates a well-balanced dressing that complements your dish perfectly.
6. Drizzle the flavorful dressing over the quinoa mixture in the large bowl. Gently fold or toss the salad ingredients together until everything is evenly distributed.
7. Let the flavors meld together for about 10 minutes.
8. Optional: Top the Mediterranean quinoa bowl with sliced avocado, a dollop of hummus, or grilled chicken or shrimp for added flavor and protein.
9. Serve the Mediterranean quinoa bowl as a wholesome and flavorful meal for two.

Nutritional breakdown per serving:
Calories: 400-450 kcal, Protein: 12 grams, Carbohydrates: 45 grams, Fat: 20 grams, Saturated Fat: 5 grams, Cholesterol: 15 milligrams, Sodium: 600 milligrams, Fiber: 8 grams, and Sugar: 4 grams.

BAKED COD WITH ROASTED VEGETABLES

- Prep Time: 15 minutes
- Total Cooking Time: 25 minutes
- Servings: 2

Ingredients:

- 2 cod fillets (6-8 ounces each)
- 1 cup cherry tomatoes
- 1 cup bell peppers (any color), sliced
- 1 cup zucchini, sliced
- 1 cup yellow squash, sliced
- 1/2 red onion, sliced
- 2 tablespoons olive oil
- 2 cloves garlic, minced
- 1 teaspoon dried thyme
- 1 teaspoon dried oregano
- Salt and pepper to taste
- Lemon wedges, for serving

Directions:

1. For perfectly cooked food with consistent results, preheat your oven to 400°F (200°C). This guarantees uniform heat distribution within the oven cavity.
2. To start, cover a baking sheet with either parchment paper or aluminum foil, then proceed to place the cod fillets on top.
3. In a large bowl, combine the cherry tomatoes, bell peppers, zucchini, yellow squash, red onion, olive oil, minced garlic, dried thyme, dried oregano, salt, and pepper. Thoroughly mix the vegetables with the seasoning to ensure an even coating.
4. Spread the vegetable mixture around the cod fillets on the baking sheet.
5. Let it bake for 20 minutes, or until the cod transforms into a dream. Look for the fish to flake effortlessly with a fork, and the vegetables to soften and develop a beautiful, slightly caramelized golden hue.
6. Remove from the oven and let it cool for a few minutes.
7. Serve the baked cod and roasted vegetables on plates, garnished with lemon wedges.
8. Enjoy the flavorful and nutritious meal for two.

Nutritional breakdown per serving:
Calories: 300-350 kcal, Protein: 30 grams, Carbohydrates: 15 grams, Fat: 15 grams, Saturated Fat: 2 grams, Cholesterol: 60 milligrams, Sodium: 300 milligrams, Fiber: 4 grams, and Sugar: 8 grams.

TURKEY AND VEGETABLE STIR-FRY

- Prep Time: 15 minutes
- Total Cooking Time: 15 minutes
- Servings: 2

Ingredients:

- 8 ounces turkey breast, thinly sliced
- 2 tablespoons soy sauce
- 1 tablespoon hoisin sauce
- 1 tablespoon honey
- 1 tablespoon cornstarch
- 2 tablespoons vegetable oil
- 2 cloves garlic, minced
- 1 teaspoon grated ginger
- 1 small onion, thinly sliced
- 1 bell pepper, thinly sliced
- 1 cup sugar snap peas
- 1 cup broccoli florets
- Salt and pepper to taste
- Cooked rice or noodles, for serving

Directions:

1. Combine the soy sauce, hoisin sauce, honey, and cornstarch in a small bowl, whisking them together. Set the mixture aside for later use.
2. Pour 1 tablespoon of vegetable oil into your pan (either a skillet or wok).
3. Place the turkey slices in the skillet and stir-fry for 3-4 minutes until fully cooked. Then, remove the turkey from the skillet and set it aside.
4. In the same skillet, warm the remaining tablespoon of vegetable oil.
5. Put the minced garlic and grated ginger into the skillet and sauté for 1 minute until fragrant.
6. Add the sliced onion, bell pepper, sugar snap peas, and broccoli florets to the skillet. Continue stir-frying for 4-5 minutes, or until the vegetables reach a tender-crisp texture.

7. Return the cooked turkey to the skillet with the vegetables.
8. Pour the sauce blend over the turkey and vegetables, then stir-fry for an extra 1-2 minutes until the sauce thickens and evenly coats all the ingredients.
9. Season with salt and pepper to taste.
10. Serve the turkey and vegetable stir-fry over cooked rice or noodles.
11. Enjoy the delicious and healthy stir-fry meal for two.

Nutritional breakdown per serving:
Calories: 350-400 kcal, Protein: 30 grams, Carbohydrates: 35 grams, Fat: 10 grams, Saturated Fat: 2 grams, Cholesterol: 60 milligrams, Sodium: 900 milligrams, Fiber: 5 grams, and Sugar: 15 grams.

CHICKEN AND VEGETABLE SKEWERS

- Prep Time: 20 minutes
- Total Cooking Time: 15 minutes
- Servings: 2

Ingredients:

- 2 boneless, skinless chicken breasts, cubed (1-inch)
- 1 red bell pepper, cut into 1-inch slices
- 1 green bell pepper, chopped (1-inch pieces)
- 1 red onion, chopped (1-inch pieces)
- 8 cherry tomatoes
- 2 tablespoons olive oil
- 2 cloves garlic, minced
- 1 teaspoon paprika
- 1 teaspoon dried oregano
- Salt and pepper to taste
- Pre-soaked wooden skewers (for 30 minutes)

Directions:

1. Preheat the grill or broiler.
2. In a large bowl, combine the cubed chicken, bell peppers, red onion, cherry tomatoes, olive oil, minced garlic, paprika, dried oregano, salt, and pepper. Toss well to coat all the ingredients with the seasoning.
3. Skewer the marinated chicken and vegetables onto the soaked wooden skewers, alternating between chicken, peppers, onion, and cherry tomatoes.
4. Place the skewers on the preheated grill or under the broiler.
5. Cook for about 7-8 minutes per side, or until the chicken is cooked through and the vegetables are slightly charred and tender.
6. Take the skewers off the grill or broiler and allow them to rest for a few minutes.
7. Serve the chicken and vegetable skewers as a delicious and colorful meal for two.

Nutritional breakdown per serving:
Calories: 300-350 kcal, Protein: 35 grams, Carbohydrates: 15 grams, Fat: 12 grams, Saturated Fat: 2 grams, Cholesterol: 80 milligrams, Sodium: 300 milligrams, Fiber: 4 grams, and Sugar: 7 grams

QUINOA AND SPINACH STUFFED PORTOBELLO MUSHROOMS

- Prep Time: 20 minutes
- Total Cooking Time: 25 minutes
- Servings: 2

Ingredients:
- 4 large Portobello mushrooms
- 1 cup cooked quinoa
- 1 cup fresh spinach, chopped
- 1/2 cup crumbled feta cheese
- 2 tablespoons grated Parmesan cheese
- 2 cloves garlic, minced
- 2 tablespoons chopped fresh basil
- 1 tablespoon olive oil
- Salt and pepper to taste

Directions:
1. Before you start assembling your dish, preheat your oven to 375°F (190°C).
2. Following the removal of the stems from the Portobello mushrooms, delicately scrape out the gills with a spoon before setting them aside.
3. In a large bowl, combine the cooked quinoa, chopped spinach, crumbled feta cheese, grated Parmesan cheese, minced garlic, chopped fresh basil, olive oil, salt, and pepper. Mix well to combine all the ingredients.
4. Spoon the quinoa and spinach mixture into the cavity of each Portobello mushroom, pressing it down gently to fill the space.
5. Lay out the stuffed mushrooms on a baking sheet, ensuring that it is lined with either parchment paper or aluminum foil.
6. Give the dish time to bake in the preheated oven for approximately 20-25 minutes, ensuring that the mushrooms become tender and the filling is thoroughly heated.
7. Remove from the oven and let it cool for a few minutes.
8. Serve the quinoa and spinach stuffed Portobello mushrooms as a delicious and nutritious meal for two.

Nutritional breakdown per serving:
Calories: 250-300 kcal, Protein: 12 grams, Carbohydrates: 30 grams, Fat: 10 grams, Saturated Fat: 4 grams, Cholesterol: 20 milligrams, Sodium: 400 milligrams, Fiber: 6 grams, and Sugar: 3 grams.

BLACKENED SHRIMP SALAD

- Prep Time: 15 minutes
- Total Cooking Time: 10 minutes
- Servings: 2

Ingredients:

For the Blackened Shrimp:

- 12 large shrimp, peeled and deveined
- 1 tablespoon olive oil
- 1 teaspoon paprika
- 1/2 teaspoon garlic powder
- 1/2 teaspoon onion powder
- 1/2 teaspoon dried thyme
- 1/2 teaspoon dried oregano
- 1/4 teaspoon cayenne pepper
- Salt and pepper to taste

For the Salad:

- 6 cups mixed salad greens
- 1 cup cherry tomatoes, halved
- 1/2 cucumber, sliced
- 1/4 red onion, thinly sliced
- 1/4 cup crumbled feta cheese
- Lemon wedges, for serving

For the Dressing:

- 2 tablespoons olive oil
- 1 tablespoon lemon juice
- 1 teaspoon Dijon mustard
- 1 clove garlic, minced
- Salt and pepper to taste

Directions:

1. In a small bowl, combine the paprika, garlic powder, onion powder, dried thyme, dried oregano, cayenne pepper, salt, and pepper to make the blackened seasoning for the shrimp.
2. Following the drying process with a paper towel, ensure an even coating by tossing the shrimp in the blackened seasoning.
3. In a large skillet over medium-high heat, heat olive oil. Add the seasoned shrimp and cook for approximately 2-3 minutes on each side until they turn pink and opaque. Once done, remove from heat and set aside.
4. Toss together in a big bowl your mixed greens, cherry tomatoes, sliced cucumber, red onion, and crumbled feta cheese.
5. In a separate small bowl, whisk together the olive oil, lemon juice, Dijon mustard, minced garlic, salt, and pepper to make the dressing.
6. After drizzling the dressing over the salad, toss it to ensure the ingredients are evenly coated.
7. Divide the salad mixture onto two plates and top each plate with the blackened shrimp.
8. Accompany the blackened shrimp salad with lemon wedges on the side to add an extra burst of citrus flavor.

Nutritional breakdown per serving:
Calories: 250-300 kcal, Protein: 20 grams, Carbohydrates: 12 grams, Fat: 15 grams, Saturated Fat: 4 grams, Cholesterol: 120 milligrams, Sodium: 500 milligrams, Fiber: 3 grams, and Sugar: 5 grams.

CHAPTER 3
DINNER

GRILLED LEMON HERB CHICKEN

- Prep Time: 15 minutes
- Total Cooking Time: 20 minutes
- Servings: 2

Ingredients:

- 2 boneless, skinless chicken breasts
- 2 tablespoons olive oil
- 2 tablespoons lemon juice
- 2 cloves garlic, minced
- 1 teaspoon dried thyme
- 1 teaspoon dried rosemary
- 1/2 teaspoon dried oregano
- Salt and pepper to taste
- Lemon slices and fresh herbs for garnish

Directions:

1. Make sure to preheat the grill to a medium-high heat setting before starting the grilling process.
2. In a small bowl, whisk together the olive oil, lemon juice, minced garlic, dried thyme, dried rosemary, dried oregano, salt, and pepper to make the marinade.
3. Position the chicken breasts in a shallow dish or a zip-top bag, ensuring they are arranged in a single layer. Thoroughly coat all sides of the chicken by pouring the marinade over it. Allow the chicken to marinate for at least 10 minutes to infuse the flavors, or refrigerate it for up to 1 hour for an enhanced taste experience.
4. Take out the chicken from the marinade and dispose of any remaining marinade.
5. Place the chicken breasts on the grill that has been preheated. Grill each side for approximately 8-10 minutes, making sure the chicken is cooked all the way through and reaches an internal temperature of 165°F (74°C).
6. Let the grilled chicken rest for a few minutes after it has been removed from the grill.
7. If desired, garnish the sliced grilled lemon herb chicken with lemon slices and fresh herbs.
8. Serve the deliciously grilled lemon herb chicken as a flavorful and satisfying meal for two.

Nutritional breakdown per serving:

Calories: 200-250 kcal, Protein: 25 grams, Carbohydrates: 2 grams, Fat: 10 grams, Saturated Fat: 10 grams, Cholesterol: 80 milligrams, Sodium: 300 milligrams, Fiber: 0 grams, and Sugar: 0 grams.

BAKED SALMON WITH DILL SAUCE

- Prep Time: 10 minutes
- Total Cooking Time: 20 minutes
- Servings: 2

Ingredients:

For the Salmon:

- 2 salmon fillets (6-8 ounces each)
- 1 tablespoon olive oil
- Salt and pepper to taste
- Lemon wedges for serving

For the Dill Sauce:

- 1/2 cup plain Greek yogurt
- 1 tablespoon fresh dill, chopped
- 1 tablespoon fresh lemon juice
- 1 clove garlic, minced
- Salt and pepper to taste

Directions:

1. To prepare for oven use, ensure that the temperature is set to 400°F (200°C) before proceeding.
2. When placing the salmon fillets on a baking sheet lined with parchment paper or aluminum foil, it's important to ensure they are evenly spaced to promote uniform cooking. This will promote even cooking and help to prevent any overlapping or crowding. Proceed by drizzling the salmon with olive oil and seasoning it with salt and pepper.
3. Bake the salmon in the preheated oven for about 15-20 minutes, or until it is cooked through and flakes easily with a fork.
4. While the salmon is in the process of baking, use this time to create the dill sauce. In a small bowl, combine Greek yogurt, chopped dill, lemon juice, minced garlic, salt, and pepper. Stir the mixture thoroughly to ensure all the ingredients are thoroughly combined.

5. Give the salmon a few minutes to rest after removing it from the oven before serving.
6. Top the baked salmon with a dollop of dill sauce and garnish with lemon wedges before serving.
7. To create a balanced meal, consider serving the salmon alongside steamed vegetables or roasted potatoes, based on your preferences.

Nutritional breakdown per serving:

Calories: 300-350 kcal, Protein: 34 grams, Carbohydrates: 3 grams, Fat: 18 grams, Saturated Fat: 3 grams, Cholesterol: 80 milligrams, Sodium: 200 milligrams, Fiber: 0 grams, and Sugar: 2 grams.

SPAGHETTI SQUASH WITH TURKEY BOLOGNESE

- Prep Time: 15 minutes
- Total Cooking Time: 1 hour 15 minutes
- Servings: 2

Ingredients:

- 1 medium spaghetti squash
- 1 tablespoon olive oil
- 1/2 pound ground turkey
- 1/2 onion, diced
- 1 carrot, diced
- 1 celery stalk, diced
- 2 cloves garlic, minced
- 1 can (14 ounces) crushed tomatoes
- 1 teaspoon dried basil
- 1 teaspoon dried oregano
- 1/2 teaspoon dried thyme
- Salt and pepper to taste
- Fresh parsley for garnish (optional)

Directions:

1. To start, ensure the oven is preheated to 400°F (200°C) before proceeding with the recipe.
2. First, cut the spaghetti squash in half lengthwise. Next, use a spoon to remove the seeds and pulp from the center.
3. Coat the exposed sides of the spaghetti squash with a thin layer of olive oil, and then arrange them on a baking sheet with the cut side facing downwards.
4. Place the spaghetti squash in the oven and cook for 45-50 minutes until the flesh is tender and can be easily separated into strands with a fork. Then, remove it from the oven and set it aside.
5. While the spaghetti squash bakes, get started on the turkey bolognese sauce by heating olive oil in a large skillet over medium heat.
6. Start by adding the ground turkey to a skillet and cook it until it browns, while using a spoon to break it up into crumbles.

7. Add the diced onion, carrot, celery, and minced garlic to the skillet. Allow the vegetables to cook until they are softened, typically taking about 5-7 minutes.
8. Next, mix in the crushed tomatoes, dried basil, dried oregano, dried thyme, salt, and pepper. Reduce the heat to low and simmer the sauce for about 20-25 minutes, allowing the flavors to meld together.
9. After cooking the spaghetti squash, utilize a fork to scrape the flesh of the squash, creating strands that resemble traditional spaghetti noodles.
10. Divide the spaghetti squash strands onto two plates. Top each plate with a generous serving of the turkey bolognese sauce.
11. Garnish with fresh parsley, if desired.
12. Serve the spaghetti squash with turkey bolognese as a delicious and healthy meal for two.

Nutritional breakdown per serving:

Calories: 300-350 kcal, Protein: 25 grams, Carbohydrates: 25 grams, Fat: 12 grams, Saturated Fat: 2 grams, Cholesterol: 60 milligrams, Sodium: 600 milligrams, Fiber: 6 grams, and Sugar: 10 grams.

VEGETABLE STIR-FRY WITH TOFU

- Prep Time: 15 minutes
- Total Cooking Time: 15 minutes
- Servings: 2

Ingredients:

- 8 ounces firm tofu, drained and cubed
- 2 tablespoons soy sauce
- 1 tablespoon cornstarch
- 2 tablespoons vegetable oil, divided
- 2 cloves garlic, minced
- 1 teaspoon grated ginger
- 1 small onion, sliced
- 1 bell pepper, sliced
- 1 cup broccoli florets
- 1 cup snap peas
- 1 carrot, julienned
- 1 cup mushrooms, sliced
- 2 tablespoons oyster sauce (optional)
- 1 tablespoon sesame oil (optional)
- Salt and pepper to taste
- Sesame seeds & green onions (optional)
- Cooked rice or noodles for serving

Directions:

1. In a bowl, combine the soy sauce and cornstarch. Add the tofu cubes and gently toss to coat them in the mixture. Set aside to marinate for 10 minutes.
2. Get 1 tablespoon vegetable oil hot in a large skillet or wok over medium-high heat.
3. Cook the marinated tofu in the skillet until golden brown and crispy on all sides, about 5-6 minutes. Then, remove it from the pan and set aside.
4. Sauté minced garlic and ginger in the pan with another tablespoon of oil until fragrant (about 1 minute).

5. Add the sliced onion, bell pepper, broccoli florets, snap peas, carrot, and mushrooms to the skillet. Cook the vegetables in the stir-fry for 4-5 minutes, until crisp-tender.

6. Return the cooked tofu to the skillet. If desired, add the oyster sauce and sesame oil for extra flavor. Toss everything together and cook for an additional 1-2 minutes to heat through.

7. Season with salt and pepper to taste.

8. Serve the vegetable stir-fry with tofu over cooked rice or noodles.

9. For a final touch, sprinkle with sesame seeds and sliced green onions (optional).

Nutritional breakdown per serving:

Calories: 300-350 kcal, Protein: 15 grams, Carbohydrates: 25 grams, Fat: 18 grams, Saturated Fat: 2 grams, Cholesterol: 0 milligrams, Sodium: 1000 milligrams, Fiber: 6 grams, and Sugar: 8 grams.

QUINOA-STUFFED ZUCCHINI BOATS

- Prep Time: 20 minutes
- Total Cooking Time: 40 minutes
- Servings: 2

Ingredients:

- 2 medium zucchini
- 1/2 cup quinoa, rinsed
- 1 cup vegetable broth
- 1 tablespoon olive oil
- 1/2 onion, diced
- 1 bell pepper, diced
- 2 cloves garlic, minced
- 1/2 teaspoon dried oregano
- 1/2 teaspoon dried basil
- 1/4 teaspoon smoked paprika
- Salt and pepper to taste
- 1/4 cup grated Parmesan cheese (optional)
- Fresh parsley for garnish (optional)

Directions:

1. For the best cooking results, it is crucial to preheat the oven to a temperature of 400 degrees Fahrenheit (200 degrees Celsius) before starting the cooking process.
2. To begin, slice the zucchini lengthwise into two equal halves. Then, take a spoon and carefully remove the flesh from the center of each zucchini half, creating a hollow shape resembling a boat. Set aside the zucchini boats for later use.
3. In a small saucepan, combine the rinsed quinoa and vegetable broth. Bring to a boil over medium-high heat. Lower heat, cover, and simmer for 15 minutes, or until quinoa is cooked through and liquid is gone. Then, remove from heat and set aside.
4. Sauté the diced onion, bell pepper, and garlic in olive oil over medium heat, releasing their fragrance, until tender (about 5-7 minutes).
5. Combine the cooked quinoa, dried oregano, dried basil, smoked paprika, salt, and pepper in the skillet. Stir thoroughly to blend all the ingredients. Let it simmer for an additional 2-3 minutes to enrich the flavors, then remove it from the heat.

6. Distribute the zucchini boats on a baking sheet. Fill them generously with the quinoa mixture, pressing it in to ensure even distribution.

7. Optional: Sprinkle grated Parmesan cheese over the stuffed zucchini boats.

8. Bake for 20-25 minutes, or until the zucchini is fork-tender and the filling is bubbly (if cheesy).

9. Take out of the oven and sprinkle with fresh parsley, for an extra touch (optional).

10. Serve the quinoa-stuffed zucchini boats as a delightful and nutritious meal for two.

Nutritional breakdown per serving:

Calories: 250-300 kcal, Protein: 10 grams, Carbohydrates: 40 grams, Fat: 8 grams, Saturated Fat: 1 grams, Cholesterol: 0 milligrams, Sodium: 500 milligrams, Fiber: 6 grams, and Sugar: 6 grams.

GRILLED SHRIMP SKEWERS WITH QUINOA SALAD

- Prep Time: 20 minutes
- Total Cooking Time: 15 minutes
- Servings: 2

Ingredients:

- 8-10 large shrimp, peeled and deveined
- 2 tablespoons olive oil
- 2 cloves garlic, minced
- 1 teaspoon paprika
- Salt and pepper to taste
- 1 cup cooked quinoa
- 1 cup cherry tomatoes, halved
- 1/2 cucumber, diced
- 1/4 cup red onion, finely chopped
- 1/4 cup fresh parsley, chopped
- Juice of 1 lemon
- 2 tablespoons extra-virgin olive oil
- Salt and pepper to taste
- Metal or soaked wooden skewers for grilling

Directions:

1. In a bowl, combine the shrimp, olive oil, minced garlic, paprika, salt, and pepper. Toss well to coat the shrimp. Set aside to marinate for 10 minutes.
2. Preheat the grill to medium-high heat.
3. While the zucchini cooks, toss together the cooled quinoa, halved cherry tomatoes, diced cucumber, red onion slivers, and chopped parsley in a large bowl.
4. In a small bowl, create a simple vinaigrette by whisking together lemon juice, olive oil, salt, and pepper. Toss the quinoa salad with the dressing to evenly coat all the ingredients. Set aside for the flavors to meld.
5. Thread the marinated shrimp onto the skewers.
6. Grill the shrimp skewers, turning once halfway through, for 2-3 minutes per side until they're opaque and pink throughout (cooked through).

7. Take the shrimp skewers off the grill and let them rest for a few minutes before serving.
8. Divide the quinoa salad onto two plates and top each plate with the grilled shrimp skewers.
9. Serve the grilled shrimp skewers with quinoa salad as a delicious and healthy meal for two.

Nutritional breakdown per serving:

Calories: 350-400 kcal, Protein: 20 grams, Carbohydrates: 30 grams, Fat: 18 grams, Saturated Fat: 2 grams, Cholesterol: 120 milligrams, Sodium: 300 milligrams, Fiber: 4 grams, and Sugar: 4 grams.

BAKED CHICKEN WITH ROASTED VEGETABLES

- Prep Time: 15 minutes
- Total Cooking Time: 40 minutes
- Servings: 2

Ingredients:

- 2 boneless, skinless chicken breasts
- 1 tablespoon olive oil
- 1 teaspoon dried thyme
- 1 teaspoon dried rosemary
- 1/2 teaspoon garlic powder
- Salt and pepper to taste
- 1 medium zucchini, sliced
- 1 red bell pepper, sliced
- 1 yellow bell pepper, sliced
- 1 small red onion, sliced
- 8-10 cherry tomatoes
- 2 tablespoons balsamic vinegar
- Fresh parsley for garnish (optional)

Directions:

1. To start, ensure the oven is preheated to 425°F (220°C) before proceeding with the recipe.
2. Position the chicken breasts on a parchment paper-lined baking sheet, and proceed to drizzle them with olive oil while sprinkling on dried thyme, dried rosemary, garlic powder, salt, and pepper. Rub the seasoning into the chicken breasts to coat them evenly.
3. In a separate bowl, combine the sliced zucchini, red and yellow bell peppers, red onion, cherry tomatoes, balsamic vinegar, salt, and pepper. Carefully toss the vegetables to guarantee that they are thoroughly coated with the balsamic vinegar and seasoning, ensuring an even distribution of flavors.
4. Arrange the seasoned vegetables around the chicken on the baking sheet.

5. Put the baking sheet with the prepared ingredients into the oven that has been preheated. Allow it to bake for approximately 25-30 minutes, or until the chicken is cooked through and the vegetables have reached a tender, slightly caramelized state.

6. Once removed from the oven, give the baking sheet some time to cool down for a few minutes before proceeding.

7. Transfer the chicken and roasted vegetables to serving plates.

8. For an optional finishing touch, garnish with fresh parsley. This herb adds a delightful pop of freshness and flavor.

9. For an optional touch, you can add a garnish of fresh parsley to enhance the dish with a burst of freshness and flavor.

Nutritional breakdown per serving:

Calories: 300-350 kcal, Protein: 30 grams, Carbohydrates: 80 grams, Fat: 12 grams, Saturated Fat: 2 grams, Cholesterol: 80 milligrams, Sodium: 300 milligrams, Fiber: 5 grams, and Sugar: 10 grams.

TURKEY CHILI

- Prep Time: 15 minutes
- Total Cooking Time: 45 minutes
- Servings: 2

Ingredients:

- 1 tablespoon olive oil
- 1/2 onion, chopped
- 1 bell pepper, chopped
- 2 cloves garlic, minced
- 8 ounces ground turkey
- 1 can (14 ounces) diced tomatoes
- 1 can (14 ounces) kidney beans, drained and rinsed
- 1 cup chicken broth
- 1 tablespoon chili powder
- 1 teaspoon ground cumin
- 1/2 teaspoon paprika
- Salt and pepper to taste
- Optional toppings: shredded cheese, chopped green onions, sour cream, avocado, etc.

Directions:

1. On medium heat, warm up olive oil in a large pot or Dutch oven.
2. Add the chopped onion, bell pepper, and minced garlic to the pot. Sauté for about 5 minutes, or until the vegetables are softened.
3. Add the ground turkey to the pot. Using a spoon, cook the meat until it is thoroughly browned and fully cooked, ensuring it is broken up into smaller pieces.
4. Mix in the diced tomatoes, kidney beans, chicken broth, chili powder, ground cumin, paprika, salt, and pepper.
5. Once the mixture reaches a boil, decrease the heat to a simmer. Cover the pot and let it simmer for around 30 minutes to allow the flavors to meld together.
6. After the 30-minute period has elapsed, remove the lid and, if necessary, season with salt and pepper.

7. Serve the turkey chili hot, topped with your preferred garnishes like shredded cheese, chopped green onions, sour cream, or avocado.

8. Enjoy the turkey chili as a hearty and flavorful meal for two.

Nutritional breakdown per serving:

Calories: 350-400 kcal, Protein: 30 grams, Carbohydrates: 30 grams, Fat: 15 grams, Saturated Fat: 3 grams, Cholesterol: 60 milligrams, Sodium: 800 milligrams, Fiber: 8 grams, and Sugar: 6 grams.

STUFFED BELL PEPPERS WITH LEAN GROUND BEEF

- Prep Time: 20 minutes
- Total Cooking Time: 1 hour
- Servings: 2

Ingredients:

- 2 large bell peppers (any color), tops removed and seeds discarded
- 1/2 pound lean ground beef
- 1/4 cup finely chopped onion
- 1 clove garlic, minced
- 1/2 cup cooked rice
- 1/2 cup diced tomatoes
- 1/4 cup tomato sauce
- 1/4 teaspoon dried oregano
- 1/4 teaspoon dried basil
- Salt and pepper to taste
- 1/4 cup shredded mozzarella cheese
- Fresh parsley for garnish (optional)

Directions:

1. To start, ensure the oven is preheated to 375°F (190°C) before proceeding with the recipe.
2. Carefully place the bell peppers in a baking dish, standing them upright on their bottoms.
3. Sauté the lean ground beef, chopped onion, and minced garlic in a skillet over medium heat, releasing their aromas, until the beef is browned and the onion is tender. Remove any excess fat if needed.
4. In a large bowl, combine the cooked ground beef mixture, cooked rice, diced tomatoes, tomato sauce, dried oregano, dried basil, salt, and pepper. Stir well to combine all the ingredients.

5. Stuff the prepared bell peppers with the ground beef mixture, pressing it in firmly for even filling and cooking. To finish, sprinkle each pepper with shredded mozzarella cheese.

6. Transfer the covered baking dish into the oven, which should already be preheated. Leave it undisturbed to bake for approximately 40 minutes until it reaches a fully cooked state.

7. For safety, let the stuffed bell peppers rest for 5-10 minutes after taking them out of the oven. This allows them to cool slightly and prevents burns.

8. Remove the peppers and cool slightly before serving.

9. Finish the dish by sprinkling with chopped fresh parsley, for an optional pop of color and flavor.

10. Serve the stuffed bell peppers with lean ground beef as a delicious and satisfying meal for two.

Nutritional breakdown per serving:

Calories: 350-400 kcal, Protein: 25 grams, Carbohydrates: 30 grams, Fat: 12 grams, Saturated Fat: 5 grams, Cholesterol: 60 milligrams, Sodium: 400 milligrams, Fiber: 5 grams, and Sugar: 8 grams.

LEMON GARLIC SHRIMP PASTA

- Prep Time: 15 minutes
- Total Cooking Time: 20 minutes
- Servings: 2

Ingredients:

- 8 ounces linguine or spaghetti
- 8-10 large shrimp, peeled and deveined
- 3 tablespoons butter, divided
- 4 cloves garlic, minced
- Zest of 1 lemon
- Juice of 1 lemon
- 1/4 cup chicken broth
- 1/4 cup heavy cream
- Salt and pepper to taste
- Fresh parsley, chopped, for garnish

Directions:

1. Start by boiling salted water and adding linguine or spaghetti. Follow the cooking time on the package to achieve al dente, which means the pasta will be cooked through but still have a slight bite. Then, drain the pasta well and set it aside.
2. Using a nonstick skillet of considerable size, melt 2 tablespoons of butter over medium heat.
3. Incorporate the minced garlic into the skillet and sauté it for approximately 1 minute, or until it becomes fragrant and releases its aroma.
4. Introduce the shrimp to the skillet and cook them for approximately 2-3 minutes on each side until they transform into a pink and opaque color. Carefully transfer the shrimp from the skillet and place them aside, ensuring that they are reserved for future use.
5. In the same skillet, add the remaining 1 tablespoon of butter, lemon zest, lemon juice, chicken broth, and heavy cream. Season with salt and pepper to taste.
6. After the mixture has come to a gentle simmer, let it cook for around 2-3 minutes until it slightly thickens, ensuring that the desired texture is attained.

7. Return the cooked shrimp to the skillet and toss to coat them in the lemon garlic sauce.

8. Incorporate the cooked linguine or spaghetti into the skillet and thoroughly toss to ensure that the pasta is evenly coated with the sauce.

9. Keep the dish cooking for an additional 1-2 minutes until it reaches a thorough level of heat, making sure that all the ingredients are evenly warmed throughout the dish.

10. Divide the lemon garlic shrimp pasta onto two plates.

11. Garnish with fresh parsley.

12. Serve the lemon garlic shrimp pasta as a flavorful and satisfying meal for two.

Nutritional breakdown per serving:

Calories: 450-500 kcal, Protein: 18 grams, Carbohydrates: 52 grams, Fat: 20 grams, Saturated Fat: 12 grams, Cholesterol: 150 milligrams, Sodium: 400 milligrams, Fiber: 3 grams, and Sugar: 2 grams.

BAKED COD WITH TOMATO-CAPER SALSA

- Prep Time: 15 minutes
- Total Cooking Time: 25 minutes
- Servings: 2

Ingredients:
- 2 cod fillets (about 6 ounces each)
- 2 tablespoons olive oil, divided
- Salt and pepper to taste
- 1 cup cherry tomatoes, halved
- 1 tablespoon capers, drained
- 1/4 red onion, finely chopped
- 2 tablespoons fresh parsley, chopped
- 1 tablespoon fresh lemon juice
- 1 clove garlic, minced

Directions:
1. To start, ensure the oven is preheated to 400°F (200°C) before proceeding with the recipe.
2. Spread the cod fillets out in a single layer on a parchment-lined baking sheet, spacing them about 1 inch apart for even cooking.
3. Drizzle the cod with 1 tablespoon olive oil and season with salt and pepper.
4. In a small mixing bowl, combine the cherry tomatoes, capers, red onion, parsley, lemon juice, minced garlic, and the remaining 1 tablespoon of olive oil. Mix well to combine.
5. Spoon the tomato-caper salsa over the cod fillets, distributing it evenly.
6. Position the prepared baking sheet inside the preheated oven and let the cod bake for approximately 12-15 minutes, or until it reaches a state of complete doneness and can be easily flaked using a fork.
7. Take the baking sheet out of the oven and let the cod rest on the wire rack for a few minutes before serving.
8. Transfer the baked cod fillets to serving plates, spooning any remaining salsa over the top.

9. Serve the baked cod with tomato-caper salsa as a flavorful and nutritious meal for two.

Nutritional breakdown per serving:

Calories: 300-350 kcal, Protein: 30 grams, Carbohydrates: 10 grams, Fat: 15 grams, Saturated Fat: 2 grams, Cholesterol: 60 milligrams, Sodium: 400 milligrams, Fiber: 2 grams, and Sugar: 4 grams.

QUINOA AND BLACK BEAN STUFFED PEPPERS

- Prep Time: 20 minutes
- Total Cooking Time: 40 minutes
- Servings: 2

Ingredients:

- 2 large bell peppers (any color), tops removed and seeds discarded
- 1/2 cup quinoa, rinsed
- 1 cup vegetable broth
- 1 tablespoon olive oil
- 1/4 cup diced onion
- 1/4 cup diced red bell pepper
- 1/4 cup diced zucchini
- 1 clove garlic, minced
- 1/2 cup black beans, drained
- 1/2 cup diced tomatoes
- 1 teaspoon chili powder
- 1/2 teaspoon ground cumin
- Salt and pepper to taste
- 1/4 cup shredded cheddar cheese (optional)
- Fresh cilantro for garnish (optional)

Directions:

1. Before you begin, make sure to preheat the oven to 375°F (190°C) for this recipe.
2. Place the bell peppers in an upright position within a baking dish.
3. Combine the quinoa and broth in a small saucepan. Place the saucepan over medium heat and heat the mixture until it comes to a boil. Then, lower the heat, cover the saucepan, and allow it to simmer for around 15 minutes. Check for the quinoa to be fully cooked and for it to have absorbed all the liquid.
4. Prepare a skillet by heating it with olive oil over medium heat. As the quinoa is cooking, allow the skillet to warm up with the olive oil.
5. Add the diced onion, red bell pepper, and zucchini to the skillet. Sauté for about 5 minutes until the vegetables are softened.

6. Include the minced garlic in the skillet and sauté it for an additional minute, making sure to stir occasionally.

7. Infuse the mixture with bold flavors by stirring in black beans, diced tomatoes, chili powder, ground cumin, salt, and pepper. Simmer for 2-3 minutes more, letting the ingredients intermingle and deepen in flavor.

8. After the quinoa cooks, transfer it to the skillet brimming with the delicious vegetable and bean mixture. Stir everything together thoroughly, creating a harmonious blend of textures and flavors.

9. Take the quinoa and black bean mixture and carefully pack it tightly into the hollowed-out bell peppers using a spoon.

10. To enhance the flavor, if desired, you can opt to sprinkle a delightful amount of shredded cheddar cheese on top of each pepper as an optional topping.

11. Cover the baking dish tightly with foil. This creates a sealed environment that traps heat and steam, promoting even cooking throughout the mixture for 20 minutes in the preheated oven.

12. Bake uncovered for an additional 5 minutes. This allows the tops to brown and the cheese to melt for a delightful finish. Aim for tender peppers for the best texture.

13. Remove from the oven and let the stuffed peppers cool for a few minutes.

14. Let the stuffed peppers cool in the oven for a few minutes.

15. Serve the quinoa and black bean stuffed peppers as a nutritious and flavorful meal for two.

Nutritional breakdown per serving:

Calories: 300-350 kcal, Protein: 12 grams, Carbohydrates: 50 grams, Fat: 8 grams, Saturated Fat: 2 grams, Cholesterol: 5 milligrams, Sodium: 600 milligrams, Fiber: 12 grams, and Sugar: 6 grams.

GRILLED VEGETABLE QUINOA BOWL

- Prep Time: 20 minutes
- Total Cooking Time: 25 minutes
- Servings: 2

Ingredients:
- 1 cup quinoa, rinsed
- 2 cups vegetable broth
- 1 zucchini, sliced lengthwise
- 1 red bell pepper, seeded and quartered
- 1 yellow bell pepper, seeded and quartered
- 1 small eggplant, sliced into rounds
- 1 red onion, sliced into thick rings
- 2 tablespoons olive oil
- Salt and pepper to taste
- 1/4 cup balsamic vinegar
- 2 tablespoons chopped fresh basil
- 2 tablespoons crumbled feta cheese (optional)
- Lemon wedges, for serving

Directions:
1. Preheat the grill to medium-high heat.
2. In a small saucepan, prep your quinoa by combining it with the broth. Bring quinoa and broth (1:2 ratio) to a boil over medium heat. Simmer covered for 15 minutes, until fluffy.
3. As the quinoa cooks, prep the vegetables by brushing them with olive oil: zucchini, red bell pepper, yellow bell pepper, eggplant, and red onion. Season with salt and pepper to taste.
4. Give the vegetables a smoky kiss on the preheated grill. Place them directly on the heat and cook for 4-5 minutes per side, or until they're tender and boast beautiful char marks. Take the vegetables off the grill and let them cool for a bit.
5. Transform the grilled vegetables into bite-sized pieces for easy eating. Add them to a large mixing bowl for easy combining later.

6. In a small bowl, whisk together the balsamic vinegar and remaining olive oil. Dress the vegetables with the sauce by tossing them together in a bowl.
7. To assemble the bowls, divide the cooked quinoa between two bowls. Top with the grilled vegetable mixture.
8. Sprinkle with chopped fresh basil and crumbled feta cheese, if desired.
9. Enhance the flavor of the grilled vegetable quinoa bowls by serving them with lemon wedges on the side, providing an additional burst of taste.

Nutritional breakdown per serving:
Calories: 350-400 kcal, Protein: 10 grams, Carbohydrates: 50 grams, Fat: 15 grams, Saturated Fat: 2 grams, Cholesterol: 0 milligrams, Sodium: 600 milligrams, Fiber: 8 grams, and Sugar: 12 grams.

CHICKEN AND VEGETABLE STIR-FRY WITH BROWN RICE

- Prep Time: 15 minutes
- Total Cooking Time: 20 minutes
- Servings: 2

Ingredients:

- 1 cup brown rice
- 2 thin-sliced boneless, skinless chicken breasts
- 2 tablespoons soy sauce
- 2 tablespoons oyster sauce
- 1 tablespoon hoisin sauce
- 1 tablespoon sesame oil
- 1 tablespoon vegetable oil
- 2 cloves garlic, minced
- 1 small onion, thinly sliced
- 1 red bell pepper, thinly sliced
- 1 cup broccoli florets
- 1 medium carrot, thinly sliced
- 1 cup snap peas, ends trimmed
- Salt and pepper to taste
- Sesame seeds for garnish (optional)
- Green onions, thinly sliced, for garnish (optional)

Directions:

1. Cook the brown rice according to the instructions provided on the package. Once it is cooked, set it aside to be used later.
2. Whisk together soy sauce, oyster sauce, and hoisin sauce in a small bowl. This easy step packs a punch and will add a delicious depth of flavor to your dish. Set aside until ready to use.
3. Apply medium-high heat to a large skillet or wok and heat both the sesame oil and vegetable oil in it.

112

4. Once the skillet is heated, add the minced garlic and cook it for approximately 30 seconds until it becomes fragrant.

5. Add the chicken strips to the skillet and cook for 4-5 minutes until they are cooked through and no longer pink. Take out the cooked chicken from the skillet and set it aside for later use.

6. Add the chopped vegetables to the party! In the same skillet, toss in the sliced onion, red bell pepper, broccoli florets, carrot slices, and snap peas. Stir-fry them for 3-4 minutes, aiming for a crisp-tender texture.

7. Place the cooked chicken back into the skillet, where the stir-fried vegetables are glistening with deliciousness.

8. Drizzle the sauce mixture over the chicken and vegetables, stir-frying for an additional 1-2 minutes to ensure even coating. Complete the dish by adding salt and pepper to taste.

9. Divide the cooked brown rice onto two plates.

10. Top the rice with the chicken and vegetable stir-fry.

11. To enhance the dish with a hint of nutty flavor and added crunch, you have the option to sprinkle sesame seeds and green onions on top, if desired.

12. Serve the chicken and vegetable stir-fry with brown rice as a delicious and satisfying meal for two.

Nutritional breakdown per serving:

Calories: 400-450 kcal, Protein: 30 grams, Carbohydrates: 50 grams, Fat: 12 grams, Saturated Fat: 2 grams, Cholesterol: 60 milligrams, Sodium: 900 milligrams, Fiber: 8 grams, and Sugar: 6 grams.

LENTIL AND VEGETABLE CURRY

- Prep Time: 15 minutes
- Total Cooking Time: 45 minutes
- Servings: 2

Ingredients:

- 1 cup dried lentils
- 2 tablespoons vegetable oil
- 1 small onion, diced
- 2 cloves garlic, minced
- 1 tablespoon fresh ginger, grated
- 1 tablespoon curry powder
- 1 teaspoon ground cumin
- 1/2 teaspoon ground turmeric
- 1/4 teaspoon cayenne pepper (optional, for heat)
- 1 can (14 ounces) diced tomatoes
- 1 cup vegetable broth
- 1 small carrot, diced
- 1 small zucchini, diced
- 1 cup cauliflower florets
- 1 cup spinach leaves
- Salt and pepper to taste
- Fresh cilantro for garnish (optional)
- Cook basmati rice or naan bread to serve alongside

Directions:
1. Rinse the lentils under cold water and set aside.
2. Set a large saucepan or Dutch oven on the stovetop and warm the vegetable oil over medium heat.
3. After adding the diced onion to the pan, sauté it for approximately 5 minutes until it turns translucent.

4. Incorporate the minced garlic and grated ginger into the mixture, stirring well, and cook for an additional minute until the aroma becomes fragrant.

5. Introduce the curry powder, ground cumin, ground turmeric, and cayenne pepper (if desired) to the pan. Stir thoroughly to ensure that the onions and spices are evenly coated.

6. Incorporate the lentils, diced tomatoes (including their juices), and vegetable broth into the pan, ensuring that all the ingredients are thoroughly combined through stirring.

7. When the mixture reaches a boiling point, lower the heat to a gentle simmer. Place a lid on the pan and allow the contents to cook undisturbed for about 25 to 30 minutes until the lentils are tender and fully cooked.

8. Add the diced carrot, zucchini, and cauliflower florets to the pan. Stir to incorporate the vegetables into the lentil mixture. Cover and simmer for an additional 10 minutes until the vegetables are tender but still have a slight bite.

9. Incorporate the spinach leaves into the pan and stir them gently. Let the spinach cook for an additional 2 to 3 minutes until it wilts.

10. Add salt and pepper to the curry according to your preference, ensuring that it is seasoned to taste.

11. Serve the lentil and vegetable curry over cooked basmati rice or with naan bread on the side.

12. Garnish with fresh cilantro, if desired.

13. Enjoy the flavorful and nutritious lentil and vegetable curry as a satisfying meal for two.

Nutritional breakdown per serving:

Calories: 350-400 kcal, Protein: 18 grams, Carbohydrates: 55 grams, Fat: 9 grams, Saturated Fat: 1 grams, Cholesterol: 0 milligrams, Sodium: 700 milligrams, Fiber: 18 grams, and Sugar: 9 grams.

BAKED EGGPLANT PARMESAN

- Prep Time: 30 minutes
- Total Cooking Time: 45 minutes
- Servings: 2

Ingredients:

- 1 large eggplant
- Salt
- 1 cup all-purpose flour
- 2 large eggs
- 1 cup breadcrumbs
- 1/2 cup grated Parmesan cheese
- 2 cups marinara sauce
- 1 cup shredded mozzarella cheese
- Fresh basil leaves, for garnish (optional)

Directions:

1. To begin, ensure that your oven is preheated to 400°F (200°C). To prevent sticking, lightly apply a coating of cooking spray or olive oil to the baking sheet.
2. Slice the eggplant into 1/4-inch thick rounds. Place the slices on a baking sheet that has been lined with paper towels, making sure to sprinkle salt evenly on both sides. Let them sit for about 15 minutes to draw out excess moisture.
3. While the eggplant is sitting, set up three shallow bowls or plates. Place the flour in one, beat the eggs in another, and combine the breadcrumbs and grated Parmesan cheese in the third.
4. After sprinkling salt on the eggplant slices, rinse them thoroughly under cold water to eliminate the salt. Next, use paper towels to pat them dry.
5. Coat each eggplant slice in flour, ensuring to shake off any excess. Subsequently, dip the coated slice into the beaten eggs, allowing any surplus to drip off. Finally, coat the slice in the breadcrumb-Parmesan mixture, pressing lightly to adhere the coating. Arrange the coated slices on the baking sheet that has been prepared.
6. Transfer the eggplant slices to the preheated oven and bake them for about 20 to 25 minutes, or until they become golden brown and crispy.

7. Take out the baking sheet from the oven and lower the oven temperature to 350°F (180°C).
8. Spread a thin coating of marinara sauce evenly across the bottom of a baking dish.
9. Place a spoonful of marinara sauce on each slice, followed by a sprinkling of shredded mozzarella cheese.
10. Repeat the process by adding another layer of eggplant, sauce, and cheese.
11. Bake the dish for 15-20 minutes, until the cheese is melted and bubbly.
12. Take the dish out of the oven, but give it a few minutes to cool down a bit.
13. Garnish with fresh basil leaves, if desired.
14. Serve the baked eggplant Parmesan as a delicious and satisfying meal for two.

Nutritional breakdown per serving:

Calories: 400-450 kcal, Protein: 20 grams, Carbohydrates: 50 grams, Fat: 15 grams, Saturated Fat: 7 grams, Cholesterol: 120 milligrams, Sodium: 900 milligrams, Fiber: 8 grams, and Sugar: 12 grams.

TURKEY MEATBALLS WITH SPAGHETTI SQUASH

- Prep Time: 20 minutes
- Total Cooking Time: 1 hour
- Servings: 2

Ingredients:

- 1 small spaghetti squash
- 1 pound ground turkey
- 1/4 cup breadcrumbs
- 1/4 cup grated Parmesan cheese
- 1/4 cup finely chopped fresh parsley
- 1 clove garlic, minced
- 1/2 teaspoon dried oregano
- 1/2 teaspoon dried basil
- 1/4 teaspoon salt
- 1/4 teaspoon black pepper
- 2 cups marinara sauce
- Fresh basil leaves, for garnish (optional)

Directions:

1. To start, ensure the oven is preheated to 400°F (200°C) before proceeding with the recipe.
2. With caution, use a knife to cut the spaghetti squash in half lengthwise, and then meticulously remove the seeds and pulp from the center using a spoon or scoop.
3. Arrange the squash halves, with the cut side facing down, on a baking sheet that has been lined with parchment paper. Place the squash halves into the oven that has been preheated and let them bake for approximately 40 to 45 minutes, or until the squash is tender and the strands can be effortlessly scraped out using a fork.
4. While the squash is in the oven, get started on preparing the turkey meatballs. Take a large mixing bowl and combine the ground turkey, breadcrumbs, grated Parmesan cheese, chopped parsley, minced garlic, dried oregano, dried basil, salt, and black pepper. Thoroughly combine the ingredients using your hands until they are evenly mixed together.
5. Shape the turkey mixture into meatballs, about 1-1.5 inches in diameter.

118

6. Warm a generously-sized non-stick skillet over medium heat. Apply a small quantity of oil or cooking spray to the skillet.
7. Arrange the meatballs in the skillet, ensuring there is enough space between them to ensure even cooking. Continue cooking the meatballs for approximately 8 to 10 minutes, making sure to turn them occasionally, until they are browned on all sides and thoroughly cooked.
8. In another saucepan, heat the marinara sauce over medium heat until it is thoroughly warmed.
9. After the spaghetti squash has finished cooking, take it out of the oven and allow it to cool for a short while. Utilize a fork to scrape the flesh of the squash, creating long strands that resemble spaghetti.
10. Divide the spaghetti squash strands onto two plates or bowls.
11. Top the squash with the cooked turkey meatballs.
12. Pour the warm marinara sauce over the meatballs.
13. Garnish with fresh basil leaves, if desired.
14. Serve the turkey meatballs with spaghetti squash as a flavorful and healthy meal for two.

Nutritional breakdown per serving:
Calories: 400-450 kcal, Protein: 30 grams, Carbohydrates: 30 grams, Fat: 18 grams, Saturated Fat: 5 grams, Cholesterol: 100 milligrams, Sodium: 900 milligrams, Fiber: 6 grams, and Sugar: 12 grams.

GRILLED PORTOBELLO MUSHROOM BURGERS

- Prep Time: 15 minutes
- Total Cooking Time: 20 minutes
- Servings: 2

Ingredients:

- 2 large Portobello mushroom caps
- 2 tablespoons balsamic vinegar
- 2 tablespoons olive oil
- 2 cloves garlic, minced
- 1 teaspoon dried thyme
- Salt and black pepper, to taste
- 4 burger buns
- 4 lettuce leaves
- 2 tomato slices
- 4 tablespoons mayonnaise (optional)
- 4 slices of cheese (optional)

Directions:

1. Preheat the grill to medium-high heat.
2. Clean the Portobello mushroom caps by gently wiping them with a damp paper towel. Remove the stems if desired.
3. In a small bowl, whisk together the balsamic vinegar, olive oil, minced garlic, dried thyme, salt, and black pepper.
4. Apply the balsamic marinade to both sides of the mushroom caps, making sure to coat them thoroughly.
5. Position the mushroom caps on the grill, ensuring that the gill side is facing down. Grill the mushrooms for approximately 4 to 5 minutes per side, or until they are tender and show grill marks.
6. While the mushrooms are grilling, prepare the burger buns. Gently grill or toast them until they are lightly toasted.
7. Assemble the burgers by spreading mayonnaise (if using) on the bottom half of each bun. Top with a lettuce leaf and a tomato slice.

8. Once the mushroom caps are cooked, remove them from the grill and place them on the prepared buns.
9. If preferred, place a slice of cheese on the upper side of each mushroom cap. The residual heat will melt the cheese.
10. Place the top half of the bun on the cheese (if using) to complete the burgers.
11. Serve the grilled Portobello mushroom burgers immediately while warm.

Nutritional breakdown per serving:

Calories: 250-300 kcal, Protein: 8 grams, Carbohydrates: 29 grams, Fat: 12 grams, Saturated Fat: 2 grams, Cholesterol: 0 milligrams, Sodium: 350 milligrams, Fiber: 4 grams, and Sugar: 6 grams.

LEMON HERB ROASTED CHICKEN WITH STEAMED BROCCOLI

- Prep Time: 15 minutes
- Total Cooking Time: 1 hour
- Servings: 2

Ingredients:

- 2 bone-in, skin-on chicken breasts
- 2 tablespoons olive oil
- 2 tablespoons freshly squeezed lemon juice
- 2 cloves garlic, minced
- 1 teaspoon dried thyme
- 1 teaspoon dried rosemary
- 1/2 teaspoon salt
- 1/4 teaspoon black pepper
- 2 cups broccoli florets
- Lemon wedges, for serving (optional)

Directions:

1. To ensure the best possible outcome, it is imperative that you preheat your oven to 425°F (220°C) prior to commencing the cooking process.
2. In a small bowl, whisk together the olive oil, lemon juice, minced garlic, dried thyme, dried rosemary, salt, and black pepper.
3. Place the chicken breasts skin-side up on a baking sheet lined with parchment paper.
4. Drizzle the lemon herb mixture over the chicken breasts, using a brush or spoon to evenly coat them.
5. After preheating the oven, carefully place the baking sheet inside and proceed to cook the chicken for a duration of 35-40 minutes. Verify that the chicken's internal temperature reaches 165°F (74°C) and observe its skin as it turns crispy and golden brown.
6. Make the most of your time while the chicken roasts! Steam the broccoli florets for a perfectly cooked side dish. Here's how: Fill a large pot with about 1 inch of water and

bring it to a boil. Then, place the steamer basket in the pot, making sure the water level stays below the basket.

7. Once the steamer basket is prepared, place the broccoli florets inside. Cover the pot and steam the broccoli for approximately 5 to 7 minutes, or until it reaches a tender consistency while retaining its vibrant green color. Conclude the process by carefully removing the pot from the heat source.

8. Out of the oven comes the chicken! Let it rest for a few minutes to lock in those delicious juices.

9. Divide the roasted chicken breasts onto two plates.

10. Serve the chicken with steamed broccoli on the side.

11. Optionally, garnish with lemon wedges for an extra burst of flavor.

12. Enjoy the lemon herb roasted chicken with steamed broccoli as a delicious and nutritious meal for two.

Nutritional breakdown per serving:

Calories: 350-400 kcal, Protein: 40 grams, Carbohydrates: 10 grams, Fat: 18 grams, Saturated Fat: 4 grams, Cholesterol: 100 milligrams, Sodium: 500 milligrams, Fiber: 4 grams, and Sugar: 2 grams.

SHRIMP AND VEGETABLE KEBABS WITH QUINOA PILAF

- Prep Time: 20 minutes
- Total Cooking Time: 25 minutes
- Servings: 2

Ingredients:

For the Shrimp and Vegetable Kebabs:

- 12 large shrimp, peeled and deveined
- 1 red bell pepper, cut into 1-inch pieces
- 1 red bell pepper, cut into 1-inch pieces
- 1 red onion, cut into wedges
- 8 cherry tomatoes
- 2 tablespoons olive oil
- 2 tablespoons freshly squeezed lemon juice
- 2 cloves garlic, minced
- 1 teaspoon dried oregano
- 1/2 teaspoon salt
- 1/4 teaspoon black pepper
- Wooden or metal skewers

For the Quinoa Pilaf:

- 1 cup quinoa
- 2 cups vegetable broth or water
- 1 tablespoon olive oil
- 1 small onion, finely chopped
- 1 carrot, finely chopped
- 1 celery stalk, finely chopped
- 1/4 cup chopped fresh parsley
- Salt and black pepper to taste

Directions:

<u>For the Shrimp and Vegetable Kebabs:</u>

1. To prevent the wooden ones from burning on the grill, it is recommended to soak them in water for a duration of 20 minutes prior to usage.
2. In a small bowl, whisk together the olive oil, lemon juice, minced garlic, dried oregano, salt, and black pepper.
3. Thread the shrimp, zucchini slices, red bell pepper pieces, red onion wedges, and cherry tomatoes onto the skewers, alternating between the ingredients.
4. Arrange the assembled kebabs in a shallow dish and generously brush them with the marinade, making sure they are thoroughly coated. Reserve some marinade for basting during grilling.
5. Preheat the grill to medium-high heat.
6. Position the kebabs on the preheated grill and grill each side for approximately 2-3 minutes. Continue cooking the kebabs until the shrimp achieve a pink and opaque color, and the vegetables reach a tender state with a hint of charred appearance. Baste the kebabs with the reserved marinade while grilling.
7. After cooking, take the kebabs off the grill and place them aside.

<u>For the Quinoa Pilaf:</u>

1. To eliminate any bitterness, rinse the quinoa under cold water using a fine-mesh sieve.
2. In a medium saucepan, heat the olive oil over medium heat. Add the chopped onion, carrot, and celery, and sauté for about 5 minutes until the vegetables are softened.
3. Introduce the rinsed quinoa to the saucepan and stir it for approximately 1 minute to lightly toast it.
4. Begin by pouring the vegetable broth or water into the saucepan and heating it until it reaches a boiling point. Next, decrease the heat to a gentle simmer, cover the saucepan, and let it simmer for a duration of 15-20 minutes until the quinoa reaches a tender consistency and absorbs all the liquid.
5. After removing the saucepan from the heat, let it sit, covered, for 5 minutes. Using a fork, gently fluff the quinoa to separate the grains.
6. To enhance the flavor, incorporate the chopped parsley into the quinoa. Then, tailor the taste by seasoning it with salt and black pepper based on your personal preference.

To Serve:

1. Divide the cooked quinoa pilaf onto two plates.
2. Place the shrimp and vegetable kebabs on top of the quinoa.
3. Serve the shrimp and vegetable kebabs with quinoa pilaf as a flavorful and nutritious meal for two.

Nutritional breakdown per serving:
Calories: 400-450 kcal, Protein: 28 grams, Carbohydrates: 150 grams, Fat: 14 grams, Saturated Fat: 2 grams, Cholesterol: 150 milligrams, Sodium: 800 milligrams, Fiber: 7 grams, and Sugar: 8 grams.

CHAPTER 4
GRAINS &
VEGETABLE

QUINOA STUFFED BELL PEPPERS

- Prep Time: 20 minutes
- Total Cooking Time: 40 minutes
- Servings: 2

Ingredients:

- 2 large bell peppers (any color)
- 1/2 cup quinoa
- 1 cup vegetable broth or water
- 1 tablespoon olive oil
- 1 small onion, finely chopped
- 1 clove garlic, minced
- 1 small zucchini, diced
- 1 small carrot, diced
- 1/2 cup black beans
- 1/2 cup corn kernels
- 1/2 teaspoon ground cumin
- 1/2 teaspoon dried oregano
- Salt and black pepper to taste
- 1/4 cup shredded cheese
- Fresh cilantro or parsley, for garnish (optional)

Directions:

1. To start, ensure the oven is preheated to 375°F (190°C) before proceeding with the recipe.
2. Trim the tops of the bell peppers by slicing them off, then proceed to delicately remove the seeds and membranes. Set aside the prepared bell peppers for future use.
3. To eliminate bitterness, rinse the quinoa under cold water using a fine-mesh sieve, ensuring to remove any impurities.
4. In a medium saucepan, bring the vegetable broth or water to a boil. Incorporate the rinsed quinoa into the saucepan, then reduce the heat to a low setting. Place a lid on the saucepan, allowing the quinoa to simmer for around 15 minutes until it is

thoroughly cooked and has absorbed all the liquid. Once done, remove the saucepan from the heat and set it aside.

5. Heat olive oil (medium heat) in your skillet. Once shimmering, toss in the chopped onion and minced garlic. Sauté for 2-3 minutes, stirring occasionally, until the onions become translucent and release their fragrant aroma.

6. Give the zucchini and carrots their turn! Add them to the skillet with the aromatics and cook for an additional 5 minutes, or until they reach a tender-crisp perfection.

7. Stir in the cooked quinoa, beans, corn, spices, and seasonings. Let it cook for 2-3 more minutes to meld the flavors, then remove from heat.

8. Stuff the peppers with the quinoa mixture, making sure every morsel of yummy gets a cozy spot.

9. Position the stuffed bell peppers in a baking dish, and if there is any surplus quinoa mixture, it can be evenly distributed around the peppers in the same dish.

10. Wrap the baking dish with foil and put it in the preheated oven for 25-30 minutes, or until the bell peppers have become tender and the filling is fully heated.

11. Take off the foil and sprinkle the shredded cheese on top of each bell pepper. Place the dish back in the oven and bake for an extra 5 minutes, or until the cheese is melted and bubbly.

12. Take out of the oven and allow the stuffed bell peppers to cool for a few minutes before serving.

13. If desired, add a finishing touch with fresh cilantro or parsley.

Nutritional breakdown per serving:
Calories: 320-350 kcal, Protein: 12 grams, Carbohydrates: 48 grams, Fat: 10 grams, Saturated Fat: 2 grams, Cholesterol: 5 milligrams, Sodium: 700 milligrams, Fiber: 10 grams, and Sugar: 10 grams.

BROWN RICE STIR-FRY

- Prep Time: 15 minutes
- Total Cooking Time: 25 minutes
- Servings: 2

Ingredients:
- 1 cup cooked brown rice
- 2 tablespoons vegetable oil, divided
- 2 cloves garlic, minced
- 1 small onion, sliced
- 1 small carrot, julienned
- 1 small bell pepper, sliced
- 1 cup broccoli florets
- 1 cup snap peas, ends trimmed
- 1/2 cup sliced mushrooms
- 2 tablespoons low-sodium soy sauce
- 1 tablespoon oyster sauce (optional)
- 1/2 teaspoon sesame oil (optional)
- Salt and black pepper to taste
- Sesame seeds, for garnish (optional)
- Green onions, chopped, for garnish (optional)

Directions:
1. Heat 1 tablespoon vegetable oil (medium-high heat) in your skillet/wok.
2. Add the fragrant minced garlic and sliced onion to the hot oil in your skillet. Sauté the onions for 2-3 minutes, until softened and fragrant.
3. Add the julienned carrot, sliced bell pepper, broccoli florets, snap peas, and sliced mushrooms to the skillet. Sauté the vegetables for 5-7 minutes, until crisp-tender.
4. Gently transfer the vegetables from the skillet to a bowl or plate. We'll add them back to the dish later.
5. Add the remaining 1 tablespoon back to the pan and heat it over medium heat.
6. Introduce the cooked brown rice to the skillet and stir-fry it for a duration of 3-4 minutes, ensuring it is thoroughly heated and the grains are properly separated.

7. Return the cooked vegetables to the skillet with the brown rice and stir to combine.

8. Combine the low-sodium soy sauce, oyster sauce (if desired), and sesame oil (if desired) in a small bowl, whisking them together. Proceed to pour the sauce over the stir-fry and toss the mixture thoroughly to ensure the rice and vegetables are evenly coated.

9. Customize the flavor by adding salt and black pepper to your liking. Keep stir-frying for an additional 2-3 minutes until all the ingredients are thoroughly combined and heated.

10. Remove the skillet from heat.

11. Serve the brown rice stir-fry in bowls or plates.

12. For an enhanced visual appeal, you may opt to add a delicate sprinkling of sesame seeds and a garnish of freshly chopped green onions, should you choose to do so.

13. Enjoy the delicious and nutritious brown rice stir-fry as a satisfying meal for two.

Nutritional breakdown per serving:

Calories: 320-350 kcal, Protein: 9 grams, Carbohydrates: 45 grams, Fat: 12 grams, Saturated Fat: 1.5 grams, Cholesterol: 0 milligrams, Sodium: 550 milligrams, Fiber: 8 grams, and Sugar: 8 grams.

LENTIL AND VEGETABLE CURRY

- Prep Time: 15 minutes
- Total Cooking Time: 40 minutes
- Servings: 2

Ingredients:

- 1 cup dried lentils (green or brown), rinsed
- 2 tablespoons vegetable oil
- 1 small onion, finely chopped
- 2 cloves garlic, minced
- 1 small carrot, diced
- 1 small bell pepper, diced
- 1 small zucchini, diced
- 1 tablespoon curry powder
- 1 teaspoon ground cumin
- 1/2 teaspoon ground turmeric
- 1/4 teaspoon cayenne pepper (optional, for heat)
- 1 can (14 ounces) diced tomatoes
- 1 can (14 ounces) coconut milk
- 1 cup vegetable broth or water
- Salt and black pepper to taste
- Fresh cilantro, chopped, for garnish (optional)
- Cooked rice or naan bread, for serving

Directions:

1. Boil 3 cups of water in your large pot. Add them to the pot after rinsing and cook for 15-20 minutes, or until they're perfectly tender but still retain their bite. Drain the cooked lentils and set them aside for now.
2. In a large skillet or Dutch oven, heat the vegetable oil over medium heat.
3. Toss the chopped onion and fragrant garlic into the hot skillet. Sauté them for 2-3 minutes, until the onion softens and turns translucent.
4. Add the diced carrot, bell pepper, and zucchini to the skillet. Sauté the vegetables for about 5 minutes until they begin to soften.

5. In a small bowl, mix together the curry powder, ground cumin, ground turmeric, and cayenne pepper (if using). Combine the spices with the vegetables in the skillet, stirring diligently to achieve a uniform coating.

6. Gently add the diced tomatoes, coconut milk, and vegetable broth or water into the mixture. Stir thoroughly to ensure proper blending.

7. Once the mixture reaches a gentle simmer, let it cook for about 15 minutes, making sure to stir occasionally during the cooking process.

8. Elevate the taste of the dish by incorporating salt and black pepper according to your desired preferences. Let the mixture continue to simmer for an extra 5 minutes to allow the flavors to blend harmoniously.

9. Remove from heat.

10. Season with salt and black pepper to taste. Continue to simmer for an additional 5 minutes to allow the flavors to meld together.

11. Remove from heat.

12. Serve the lentil and vegetable curry over cooked rice or with naan bread.

13. Garnish with fresh chopped cilantro if desired.

14. Enjoy the flavorful and hearty lentil and vegetable curry as a delicious meal for two.

Nutritional breakdown per serving:

Calories: 380-420 kcal, Protein: 15 grams, Carbohydrates: 47 grams, Fat: 18 grams, Saturated Fat: 14 grams, Cholesterol: 0 milligrams, Sodium: 600 milligrams, Fiber: 16 grams, and Sugar: 10 grams.

MEDITERRANEAN COUSCOUS SALAD

- Prep Time: 15 minutes
- Total Cooking Time: 15 minutes
- Servings: 2

Ingredients:

- 1 cup couscous
- 1 cup vegetable broth or water
- 2 tablespoons extra virgin olive oil
- 2 tablespoons lemon juice
- 1 clove garlic, minced
- 1 teaspoon Dijon mustard
- Salt and black pepper to taste
- 1 cup cherry tomatoes, halved
- 1/2 English cucumber, diced
- 1/4 cup halved Kalamata olives
- 1/4 cup crumbled feta cheese
- 2 tablespoons chopped fresh parsley
- 2 tablespoons chopped fresh mint
- 2 tablespoons chopped fresh basil

Directions:

1. In a small saucepan, heat your preferred broth (or water) until it reaches a boiling point. Take the saucepan off the heat, add the couscous, cover it, and let it sit undisturbed for 5 minutes to achieve a delightful and fluffy texture.
2. Gently loosen the cooked couscous using a fork to separate the grains, then transfer it to a spacious mixing bowl.
3. In a separate small bowl, whisk together the extra virgin olive oil, lemon juice, minced garlic, Dijon mustard, salt, and black pepper to make the dressing.
4. Drizzle the dressing evenly over the cooked couscous and toss thoroughly to ensure all the grains are coated.

5. Add the cherry tomatoes, diced cucumber, Kalamata olives, crumbled feta cheese, chopped fresh parsley, chopped fresh mint, and chopped fresh basil to the bowl with the couscous. Carefully mix all the ingredients together until thoroughly combined.

6. Taste and adjust the seasoning if needed.

7. Allow the Mediterranean couscous salad to rest for a few minutes to let the flavors meld together.

8. Serve the salad as a refreshing and nutritious meal for two.

Nutritional breakdown per serving:

Calories: 350-380 kcal, Protein: 9 grams, Carbohydrates: 45 grams, Fat: 15 grams, Saturated Fat: 4 grams, Cholesterol: 15 milligrams, Sodium: 480 milligrams, Fiber: 5 grams, and Sugar: 4 grams.

SPAGHETTI SQUASH PRIMAVERA

- Prep Time: 15 minutes
- Total Cooking Time: 1 hour 15 minutes
- Servings: 2

Ingredients:

- 1 medium spaghetti squash
- 2 tablespoons olive oil
- 2 cloves garlic, minced
- 1 small onion, diced
- 1 small carrot, thinly sliced
- 1 small bell pepper, thinly sliced
- 1 small zucchini, thinly sliced
- 1 cup cherry tomatoes, halved
- 1/2 cup vegetable broth
- 1 teaspoon dried Italian seasoning
- Salt and black pepper to taste
- Grated Parmesan cheese, for garnish (optional)
- Fresh basil leaves, torn, for garnish (optional)

Directions:

1. Ensure the oven is set to 400°F (200°C) while preparing the ingredients.
2. Cut the spaghetti squash in half lengthwise, and then proceed to scoop out the seeds and pulp.
3. Add a generous drizzle of 1 tablespoon of olive oil to the exposed sides of the spaghetti squash, and then generously season with salt and black pepper to elevate its flavor.
4. Allow them to roast in the preheated oven for around 40-45 minutes, or until the squash reaches a tender consistency and the flesh can be effortlessly scraped with a fork.
5. Using a fork, gently scrape the flesh of the squash to create long, tender strands that resemble spaghetti. Set them aside for now.
6. Simmer the remaining tablespoon of olive oil in the pan over medium.

7. Toss the minced garlic and diced onion into the skillet and cook them for 2-3 minutes, until the onion softens and turns translucent.

8. Add the sliced carrot, bell pepper, and zucchini to the skillet. Sauté the vegetables for about 5 minutes until they begin to soften.

9. Stir in the halved cherry tomatoes, vegetable broth, and dried Italian seasoning. Season with salt and pepper to taste. Let this cook for another 5 minutes, until the vegetables are tender and the flavors come together.

10. Incorporate the spaghetti squash into the pan and toss well to coat the strands with the seasoned vegetables.

11. Continue to cook for a few more minutes until the spaghetti squash is heated through.

12. Remove from heat.

13. Serve the spaghetti squash primavera in bowls or plates.

14. For an extra touch, sprinkle with grated Parmesan cheese and tear some fresh basil leaves over the top.

15. Enjoy the light and flavorful spaghetti squash primavera as a healthy meal for two.

Nutritional breakdown per serving:

Calories: 230-250 kcal, Protein: 4 grams, Carbohydrates: 27 grams, Fat: 13 grams, Saturated Fat: 2 grams, Cholesterol: 0 milligrams, Sodium: 360 milligrams, Fiber: 6 grams, and Sugar: 11 grams.

QUINOA AND BLACK BEAN SALAD

- Prep Time: 15 minutes
- Total Cooking Time: 20 minutes
- Servings: 2

Ingredients:

- 1/2 cup quinoa
- 1 cup vegetable broth or water
- 15 oz rinsed & drained black beans
- 1 cup cherry tomatoes, halved
- 1/2 cup diced red bell pepper
- 1/2 cup diced cucumber
- 2 green onions, thinly sliced
- 1/4 cup chopped fresh cilantro
- 2 tablespoons fresh lime juice
- 2 tablespoons extra virgin olive oil
- 1 clove garlic, minced
- 1/2 teaspoon ground cumin
- Salt and black pepper to taste
- Avocado slices, for garnish (optional)

Directions:

1. Run cold water over the quinoa to remove the saponins.
2. In a small saucepan, heat your choice of vegetable broth or water until boiling. Stir in the rinsed quinoa and reduce heat to maintain a low simmer.
3. Simmer, covered, for 15 minutes. The quinoa is done when fluffy and the liquid is gone. Then, remove from heat and let cool.
4. In a large mixing bowl, combine the cooked quinoa, black beans, cherry tomatoes, diced red bell pepper, diced cucumber, sliced green onions, and chopped cilantro.
5. For the dressing, whisk together lime juice, olive oil, minced garlic, cumin, salt, and black pepper in a small bowl.

6. Dress the quinoa and black bean mixture by pouring the prepared dressing over it. Give everything a good toss to coat the quinoa and black beans evenly with the dressing.
7. Taste and adjust the seasoning if needed.
8. Let the quinoa and black bean salad sit for a few minutes to allow the flavors to meld together.
9. Serve the salad in bowls or plates.
10. Garnish with avocado slices if desired.
11. Enjoy the nutritious and flavorful quinoa and black bean salad as a satisfying meal for two.

Nutritional breakdown per serving:

Calories: 350-380 kcal, Protein: 12 grams, Carbohydrates: 46 grams, Fat: 15 grams, Saturated Fat: 2 grams, Cholesterol: 0 milligrams, Sodium: 420 milligrams, Fiber: 12 grams, and Sugar: 5 grams.

BARLEY AND VEGETABLE SOUP

- Prep Time: 15 minutes
- Total Cooking Time: 1 hour
- Servings: 2

Ingredients:

- 1/2 cup pearl barley
- 4 cups vegetable broth or water
- 1 tablespoon olive oil
- 1 small onion, diced
- 2 cloves garlic, minced
- 2 medium carrots, diced
- 2 celery stalks, diced
- 1 small zucchini, diced
- 1 cup diced tomatoes (fresh or canned)
- 1 teaspoon dried thyme
- 1 teaspoon dried oregano
- Salt and black pepper to taste
- Fresh parsley, chopped, for garnish (optional)

Directions:
1. Wash the pearl barley in cold water. Drain and set it aside for later use.
2. Heat the vegetable broth (or water) in a large pot until boiling. Stir in the rinsed pearl barley and simmer on low heat.
3. Simmer for 40-45 minutes with the pot covered, stirring occasionally, until the barley is tender.
4. Sauté the diced onion and minced garlic for 2-3 minutes. You'll want them softened and aromatic before adding the next ingredients.
5. Add the diced onion and minced garlic to the pot. Sauté for 2-3 minutes until the onion becomes translucent and fragrant.
6. Add the diced carrots, celery, zucchini, and diced tomatoes to the pot. Stir well to combine.

7. Next, sprinkle the dried thyme and oregano over the vegetables. Give it a hit of flavor with salt and freshly ground black pepper. Season to your preference.

8. Sauté the vegetables over medium heat for 5-7 minutes, stirring occasionally, until they reach a tender-crisp texture.

9. Once the barley is cooked, drain any excess liquid and add the cooked barley to the pot with the vegetables.

10. Stir everything together to combine. For a thinner soup, feel free to stir in some water or vegetable broth, a little at a time, until it reaches your preferred consistency.

11. Simmer the soup for another 10-15 minutes. Simmering for a bit longer unlocks the vegetables' flavors, infusing the broth with a rich depth.

12. Taste and adjust the seasoning if needed.

13. Remove from heat.

14. Serve the barley and vegetable soup in bowls.

15. Garnish with fresh chopped parsley if desired.

16. Enjoy the hearty and nourishing barley and vegetable soup as a comforting meal for two.

Nutritional breakdown per serving:
Calories: 260-280 kcal, Protein: 8 grams, Carbohydrates: 50 grams, Fat: 5 grams, Saturated Fat: 1 grams, Cholesterol: 0 milligrams, Sodium: 800 milligrams, Fiber: 11 grams, and Sugar: 7 grams.

WILD RICE PILAF WITH ROASTED VEGETABLES

- Prep Time: 15 minutes
- Total Cooking Time: 1 hour 15 minutes
- Servings: 2

Ingredients:
- 1/2 cup wild rice
- 1 1/2 cups vegetable broth or water
- 1 cup diced butternut squash
- 1 cup Brussels sprouts, halved
- 1 small red onion, diced
- 2 cloves garlic, minced
- 2 tablespoons olive oil
- 1 teaspoon dried thyme
- Salt and black pepper to taste
- 1/4 cup chopped pecans (optional)
- Fresh parsley, chopped, for garnish (optional)

Directions:
1. Wash the wild rice with cold water to remove any impurities. Drain it and set aside for later use.
2. Bring your chosen liquid, vegetable broth or water, to a boil in a medium saucepan. Once boiling, add the rinsed wild rice and lower the heat to maintain a gentle simmer.
3. Simmer the rinsed wild rice in covered saucepan with vegetable broth (or water) for 45-50 minutes, until tender and the liquid is absorbed. Remove from heat and let rest for a few minutes.
4. Ensure the oven is set to 400°F (200°C) while preparing the ingredients.
5. In a large baking sheet, combine the diced butternut squash, halved Brussels sprouts, diced red onion, minced garlic, olive oil, dried thyme, salt, and black pepper. Give everything a good toss to evenly coat the vegetables with the oil and seasonings.
6. Spread the vegetables out in a single layer on the baking sheet.

7. Roast the vegetables for 25-30 minutes in the preheated oven, turning them occasionally, until tender and nicely browned. To ensure even cooking, gently stir the vegetables once or twice during their roasting time.
8. While the vegetables are roasting, fluff the cooked wild rice with a fork.
9. Roast the vegetables until tender-crisp and golden brown, about 25-30 minutes. Remove them from the oven and let cool for a few minutes before serving.
10. In a serving bowl, combine the cooked wild rice and roasted vegetables. Toss gently to mix them together.
11. If desired, sprinkle chopped pecans over the pilaf for added crunch and flavor.
12. Taste and adjust the seasoning if needed.
13. Garnish with fresh chopped parsley if desired.
14. Serve the wild rice pilaf with roasted vegetables as a delicious and wholesome meal for two.

Nutritional breakdown per serving:

Calories: 320-350 kcal, Protein: 7 grams, Carbohydrates: 45 grams, Fat: 15 grams, Saturated Fat: 2 grams, Cholesterol: 0 milligrams, Sodium: 520 milligrams, Fiber: 7 grams, and Sugar: 7 grams.

WHOLE WHEAT PASTA PRIMAVERA

- Prep Time: 15 minutes
- Total Cooking Time: 20 minutes
- Servings: 2

Ingredients:

- 6 ounces whole wheat pasta
- 1 tablespoon olive oil
- 2 cloves garlic, minced
- 1 small onion, thinly sliced
- 1 small carrot, julienned
- 1 small zucchini, julienned
- 1 cup broccoli florets
- 1/2 cup cherry tomatoes, halved
- 1/2 cup sliced bell peppers (any color)
- 1/2 cup fresh or frozen peas
- 1/2 cup vegetable broth
- 1/4 cup grated Parmesan cheese (optional)
- Salt and black pepper to taste
- Fresh basil or parsley, chopped, for garnish (optional)

Directions:

1. Boil the whole wheat pasta in plenty of water, following the package guide, until al dente. Once drained, toss the pasta with a little olive oil to prevent sticking. Keep it warm until serving time.
2. Gently heat olive oil in a large skillet or sauté pan over medium heat.
3. Let the minced garlic and sliced onion soften in the skillet. Cook them over medium heat for 2-3 minutes, giving them a stir now and then, until they turn translucent and slightly softened.
4. Add the julienned carrot, julienned zucchini, broccoli florets, cherry tomatoes, sliced bell peppers, and peas to the pan. Stir well to combine.
5. Pour the vegetable broth into the pan. Cover and cook for 5-7 minutes, or until the vegetables are tender-crisp.

6. Season the vegetables generously with salt and freshly cracked black pepper.
7. Gently fold the cooked pasta into the skillet with the seasoned vegetables. Toss everything until well combined.
8. Sauté for another 2-3 minutes until the pasta is warmed through.
9. For a cheesy finish, sprinkle grated Parmesan cheese over the pasta primavera and toss to coat.
10. Taste and adjust the seasoning if needed.
11. Remove from heat.
12. Serve the whole wheat pasta primavera in bowls or plates.
13. Garnish with chopped fresh basil or parsley, depending on your taste.
14. Enjoy the nutritious and flavorful whole wheat pasta primavera as a delightful meal for two.

Nutritional breakdown per serving:

Calories: 350-380 kcal, Protein: 12 grams, Carbohydrates: 60 grams, Fat: 9 grams, Saturated Fat: 1 grams, Cholesterol: 0 milligrams, Sodium: 400 milligrams, Fiber: 10 grams, and Sugar: 5 grams.

QUINOA AND SPINACH STUFFED PORTOBELLO MUSHROOMS

- Prep Time: 15 minutes
- Total Cooking Time: 30 minutes
- Servings: 2

Ingredients:

- 2 large Portobello mushrooms
- 1/2 cup quinoa
- 1 cup vegetable broth or water
- 1 tablespoon olive oil
- 2 cloves garlic, minced
- 2 cups fresh spinach, chopped
- 1/4 cup diced red bell pepper
- 1/4 cup diced onion
- 1/4 cup crumbled feta cheese (optional)
- 2 tablespoons grated Parmesan cheese (optional)
- Salt and black pepper to taste
- Fresh parsley, chopped, for garnish (optional)

Directions:

1. Ensure the oven is set to 375°F (190°C) while preparing the ingredients.
2. Clean the Portobello mushrooms. Remove the stems and carefully scrape the gills from the portobello mushrooms with a spoon. Once clean, set the caps aside for use later.
3. In a fine-mesh strainer, rinse the quinoa under cold water. Drain well.
4. Heat the vegetable broth or water in a medium saucepan until it boils. Stir in the rinsed quinoa and lower the heat to low.
5. Let the covered quinoa simmer for 15 minutes, or until the liquid absorbs and the grains are cooked through. Then, take the pot off the heat and let it rest for a few minutes.
6. While the quinoa simmers, heat olive oil in a skillet over medium heat.

7. Add the minced garlic, diced red bell pepper, and diced onion to the skillet. Sauté for 2-3 minutes until the vegetables are softened.

8. Incorporate the chopped spinach and cook for 2-3 minutes, till softened.

9. Taste the vegetable mixture and season with salt and black pepper as desired.

10. Fluff the cooked quinoa in a bowl and add the sautéed vegetables. Gently fold everything together to combine.

11. Prep a baking sheet by laying down parchment paper. Add the portobello mushrooms on top.

12. Divide the quinoa and vegetable mixture evenly between the mushroom caps, filling them in the center.

13. If desired, sprinkle crumbled feta cheese and grated Parmesan cheese over the stuffed mushrooms.

14. Bake the portobello mushrooms for 15-20 minutes in the preheated oven. They're done when tender and any cheese is melted and lightly browned.

15. Take the portobellos out of the oven and let them sit for a few minutes to cool down.

16. Garnish with fresh chopped parsley if desired.

17. Serve the quinoa and spinach stuffed Portobello mushrooms as a delicious and satisfying meal for two.

Nutritional breakdown per serving:

Calories: 250-280 kcal, Protein: 12 grams, Carbohydrates: 30 grams, Fat: 10 grams, Saturated Fat: 3 grams, Cholesterol: 10 milligrams, Sodium: 500 milligrams, Fiber: 6 grams, and Sugar: 4 grams.

VEGETABLE FRIED RICE

- Prep Time: 15 minutes
- Total Cooking Time: 20 minutes
- Servings: 2

Ingredients:
- 1 cup cooked white rice (preferably cooled or day-old)
- 2 tablespoons vegetable oil
- 2 cloves garlic, minced
- 1 small onion, diced
- 1 medium carrot, diced
- 1/2 cup frozen peas
- 1/2 cup diced bell peppers
- 2 green onions, sliced
- 2 tablespoons soy sauce
- 1 tablespoon oyster sauce (optional)
- 1/2 teaspoon sesame oil
- Salt and black pepper to taste
- 2 eggs, lightly beaten
- Chopped fresh cilantro or parsley for an optional garnish

Directions:
1. Get a large skillet or wok going over medium-high heat. Add 1 tablespoon of vegetable oil.
2. Throw in the minced garlic and diced onion. Sauté for 2-3 minutes, until the onions soften and become fragrant.
3. Sauté the vegetables for 3-4 minutes, stirring now and then, until they're crisp-tender.
4. Push the vegetables to one side of the skillet, creating an empty space.
5. In the empty space, add the beaten eggs. Scramble the eggs until they are cooked through.
6. Mix the scrambled eggs with the vegetables in the skillet.
7. Scrape the cooked white rice into the skillet and gently fold it in with a spatula, breaking up any clumps.

8. Lightly season with salt and pepper. Since soy sauce contributes saltiness, taste as you go to avoid overdoing it.

9. Season with salt and black pepper to taste. Be mindful of the saltiness of the soy sauce.

10. Continue stir-frying for another 2-3 minutes until the rice is heated through.

11. Throw in the sliced green onions and stir everything together.

12. Taste and adjust the seasoning if needed.

13. Remove from heat.

14. Serve the vegetable fried rice in bowls or plates.

15. For a pop of freshness, finish with chopped cilantro or parsley (optional).

16. Enjoy the flavorful and satisfying vegetable fried rice as a delightful meal for two.

Nutritional breakdown per serving:

Calories: 350-380 kcal, Protein: 11 grams, Carbohydrates: 49 grams, Fat: 14 grams, Saturated Fat: 2 grams, Cholesterol: 105 milligrams, Sodium: 850 milligrams, Fiber: 5 grams, and Sugar: 7 grams.

BULGUR SALAD WITH ROASTED VEGETABLES

- Prep Time: 15 minutes
- Total Cooking Time: 40 minutes
- Servings: 2

Ingredients:

- 1/2 cup bulgur wheat
- 1 cup vegetable broth or water
- 1 small eggplant, diced
- 1 small zucchini, diced
- 1 red bell pepper, diced
- 1 small red onion, thinly sliced
- 2 tablespoons olive oil
- 1 teaspoon ground cumin
- 1/2 teaspoon paprika
- 1/4 teaspoon cayenne pepper (optional for spice)
- Salt and black pepper to taste
- 2 tablespoons lemon juice
- 2 tablespoons fresh parsley, chopped
- 2 tablespoons fresh mint, chopped
- 2 tablespoons crumbled feta cheese (optional)

Directions:

1. While you're getting the ingredients ready, preheat your oven to 400°F (200°C).
2. Rinse the bulgur wheat under cold water and drain well.
3. Heat vegetable broth or water in a saucepan until boiling. Next, add the rinsed bulgur wheat. Reduce heat to low, cover, and simmer for 15 minutes. Once cooked through, remove from heat and let it fluff for a few minutes.
4. On a baking sheet, arrange the diced eggplant, zucchini, red bell pepper, and thinly sliced red onion.
5. Dress the vegetables on the baking sheet with olive oil. Spice things up with ground cumin, paprika, and cayenne pepper (optional). Season with salt and pepper, then give everything a good toss to coat the veggies evenly in the oil and spices.

6. Bake the vegetables for 20-25 minutes in the preheated oven. Aim for tender and slightly browned, giving them a toss or two halfway through to ensure even cooking.
7. In a large bowl, lighten up the cooked bulgur wheat with a fork and fold in the roasted vegetables.
8. Add the lemon juice, fresh chopped parsley, and fresh chopped mint to the bowl. Toss everything together to mix well.
9. Taste and adjust the seasoning if needed.
10. For an extra layer of flavor, add crumbled feta cheese to the salad (optional). Toss gently to incorporate.
11. Divide the bulgur salad with roasted vegetables into two serving bowls or plates.
12. Enjoy this healthy and flavorful meal for two! Serve the bulgur wheat salad warm or at room temperature.

Nutritional breakdown per serving:

Calories: 280-320 kcal, Protein: 8 grams, Carbohydrates: 40 grams, Fat: 14 grams, Saturated Fat: 2 grams, Cholesterol: 0 milligrams, Sodium: 400 milligrams, Fiber: 9 grams, and Sugar: 8 grams.

FARRO AND ROASTED BEET SALAD

- Prep Time: 15 minutes
- Total Cooking Time: 1 hour and 15 minutes
- Servings: 2

Ingredients:
- 2 medium beets, peeled and diced
- 1 cup farro
- 2 cups vegetable broth or water
- 2 tablespoons olive oil, divided
- 2 cups baby spinach or mixed greens
- 1/4 cup crumbled goat cheese
- 1/4 cup chopped walnuts
- 2 tablespoons balsamic vinegar
- Salt and black pepper to taste

Directions:
1. While you're getting the ingredients ready, preheat your oven to 400°F (200°C).
2. Spread the diced beets on a baking sheet. Toss everything together with 1 tablespoon olive oil, salt, and pepper, making sure the beets are evenly coated.
3. Roast the beets for 30-35 minutes in the preheated oven, aiming for tender and slightly caramelized. Once done, take them out and let them cool.
4. Add the farro and your choice of vegetable broth or water to a medium saucepan. Heat the pot over medium-high heat until it reaches a rolling boil.
5. Let it come to a boil, then reduce heat to low setting. Simmer for 25-30 minutes, covered. The farro is done when it's tender and all the liquid is gone. Remove from heat and let it rest for a few minutes.
6. In a large mixing bowl, combine the cooked farro, roasted beets, baby spinach or mixed greens, crumbled goat cheese, and chopped walnuts.
7. For a flavorful salad, toss all the ingredients with the dressing until well combined.
8. Take a bite to check the seasoning. Feel free to add pinches of salt and pepper to your taste.
9. Divide the farro and roasted beet salad into two serving bowls or plates.

10. Whether you crave a cool and crisp salad or a more comforting option, this dish delivers! Serve it chilled or at room temperature.

Nutritional breakdown per serving:

Calories: 450-500 kcal, Protein: 15 grams, Carbohydrates: 55 grams, Fat: 22 grams, Saturated Fat: 4 grams, Cholesterol: 10 milligrams, Sodium: 500 milligrams, Fiber: 10 grams, and Sugar: 8 grams.

QUINOA AND VEGETABLE STIR-FRY

- Prep Time: 15 minutes
- Total Cooking Time: 25 minutes
- Servings: 2

Ingredients:

- 1/2 cup quinoa
- 1 cup vegetable broth or water
- 2 tablespoons soy sauce
- 1 tablespoon sesame oil
- 1 tablespoon rice vinegar
- 1 tablespoon honey or maple syrup
- 1 tablespoon cornstarch
- 2 tablespoons vegetable oil
- 2 cloves garlic, minced
- 1 small onion, sliced
- 1 medium carrot, julienned
- 1 bell pepper, thinly sliced
- 1 cup broccoli florets
- 1 cup snap peas, ends trimmed
- Salt and black pepper to taste
- Sesame seeds, green onions (optional)

Directions:

1. Rinse the quinoa under cold water and drain well.
2. Heat vegetable broth (or water) to a boil in a medium saucepan. Add the rinsed quinoa, then lower the heat to low. Pop the lid on and simmer for 15 minutes. The quinoa is ready when it's nice and fluffy. Remove from heat and let it rest for a few minutes.
3. In a small bowl, make the dressing: whisk soy sauce, sesame oil, rice vinegar, and your preferred sweetener (honey or maple syrup). Add the cornstarch and set aside.
4. Get a large skillet or wok going over medium-high heat.

5. Toss in the garlic and onion. Sauté for 2-3 minutes, looking for softened onions and a delicious aroma.
6. Add the julienned carrot, sliced bell pepper, broccoli florets, and snap peas to the skillet. Sauté for 4-5 minutes, or until the vegetables reach a tender-crisp perfection.
7. Take a moment to taste the dish, and then make any necessary adjustments to the seasoning with salt and pepper to suit your personal preferences.
8. Push the vegetables to one side of the skillet, creating an empty space.
9. Pour the prepared sauce into the empty space. Stir the sauce until it thickens.
10. Mix the sauce with the vegetables in the skillet.
11. Add the cooked quinoa to the skillet. Toss everything together to coat the quinoa and vegetables with the sauce.
12. Keep stir-frying for an additional 2-3 minutes until the quinoa is thoroughly heated.
13. Taste and adjust the seasoning if needed.
14. Remove from heat.
15. Divide the quinoa and vegetable stir-fry into two serving bowls or plates.
16. If you like, you can add a garnish of sesame seeds and chopped green onions.
17. Serve the delicious and nutritious quinoa and vegetable stir-fry as a satisfying meal for two.

Nutritional breakdown per serving:
Calories: 400-450 kcal, Protein: 10 grams, Carbohydrates: 55 grams, Fat: 18 grams, Saturated Fat: 2 grams, Cholesterol: 0 milligrams, Sodium: 900 milligrams, Fiber: 8 grams, and Sugar: 12 grams.

BARLEY RISOTTO WITH MUSHROOMS

- Prep Time: 10 minutes
- Total Cooking Time: 45 minutes
- Servings: 2

Ingredients:
- 1 tablespoon olive oil
- 1 small onion, finely chopped
- 2 cloves garlic, minced
- 8 oz sliced mushrooms
- 1 cup pearled barley
- 3 cups vegetable broth or chicken broth
- 1/4 cup grated Parmesan cheese (optional)
- Salt and black pepper to taste
- Fresh parsley, chopped (for garnish)

Directions:
1. Get your large skillet ready by heating a drizzle of olive oil over medium heat.
2. Toss the chopped onion into the hot skillet and sauté for 2-3 minutes, until it turns translucent.
3. Once the onions are softened, stir in the fragrant minced garlic and sliced mushrooms. Continue cooking for about 5 minutes. You'll know the mushrooms are ready when they've softened up and boast a beautiful light brown color.
4. Add it to the skillet with the aromatics and cook for 1-2 minutes, stirring regularly. Watch as the barley gets a delightful toasty coating from the oil.
5. The barley needs some liquid to cook. After toasting, deglaze the pan with 1 cup of your preferred broth, vegetable or chicken.
6. Once the liquid is mostly absorbed, add another cup of broth. Continue this process, adding the remaining broth in increments, stirring occasionally, until the barley is cooked and tender. This should take about 30-35 minutes.
7. To personalize your dish, consider stirring in some grated Parmesan cheese and seasoning it with salt and black pepper to your liking. Mix thoroughly until the cheese is melted and the risotto reaches a creamy consistency.
8. Remove from heat and let it rest for a few minutes.

9. Divide the barley risotto with mushrooms into two serving bowls or plates.
10. Garnish with fresh chopped parsley.
11. Serve the flavorful and hearty barley risotto as a delightful meal for two.

Nutritional breakdown per serving:

Calories: 350-400 kcal, Protein: 12 grams, Carbohydrates: 65 grams, Fat: 7 grams, Saturated Fat: 1 grams, Cholesterol: 0 milligrams, Sodium: 700 milligrams, Fiber: 12 grams, and Sugar: 4 grams.

MEDITERRANEAN BULGUR BOWL

- Prep Time: 15 minutes
- Total Cooking Time: 25 minutes
- Servings: 2

Ingredients:

- 1 cup bulgur wheat
- 2 cups vegetable broth or water
- 1 tablespoon olive oil
- 2 cloves garlic, minced
- 1 small red onion, thinly sliced
- 1 cup cherry tomatoes, halved
- 1 cucumber, diced
- 1/4 cup Kalamata olives, pitted and halved
- 1/4 cup crumbled feta cheese
- 2 tablespoons chopped fresh parsley
- Juice of 1 lemon
- Salt and black pepper to taste

Optional Toppings:

- Hummus
- Tzatziki sauce
- Grilled chicken or tofu

Directions:

1. Rinse the bulgur wheat under cold water and drain well.
2. Incorporate the rinsed bulgur wheat, lower the heat to a gentle simmer, cover the pot, and let it cook for approximately 15 minutes or until the bulgur becomes tender and absorbs all the liquid. Remove from heat and let it rest for a few minutes.
3. Every dish has hidden flavor waiting to be unlocked. A touch of salt and pepper can be the key.
4. Combine the minced garlic and sliced red onion in the skillet, and sauté for 3-4 minutes until the onion achieves a soft, translucent texture.

5. Let the cherry tomatoes join the skillet and allow them to cook for an extra 2 minutes until they reach a softened state.

6. In a large mixing bowl, combine the cooked bulgur wheat, sautéed onion and tomato mixture, diced cucumber, Kalamata olives, crumbled feta cheese, chopped fresh parsley, and lemon juice.

7. Toss everything together until well combined.

8. Start with a pinch of salt and a sprinkle of black pepper, then adjust to your taste preferences.

9. Divide the Mediterranean bulgur mixture into two serving bowls.

10. If desired, top the bowls with hummus, tzatziki sauce, and grilled chicken or tofu.

11. Serve the vibrant and flavorful Mediterranean bulgur bowl as a nourishing meal for two.

Nutritional breakdown per serving:

Calories: 350-400 kcal, Protein: 12 grams, Carbohydrates: 55 grams, Fat: 12 grams, Saturated Fat: 4 grams, Cholesterol: 15 milligrams, Sodium: 600 milligrams, Fiber: 10 grams, and Sugar: 8 grams.

VEGETABLE AND CHICKPEA CURRY WITH BROWN RICE

- Prep Time: 15 minutes
- Total Cooking Time: 30 minutes
- Servings: 2

Ingredients:

- 1 cup brown rice
- 2 cups water
- 1 tablespoon vegetable oil
- 1 small onion, finely chopped
- 2 cloves garlic, minced
- 1 tablespoon grated fresh ginger
- 1 tablespoon curry powder
- 1/2 teaspoon ground cumin
- 1/2 teaspoon ground turmeric
- 1/4 teaspoon cayenne pepper (optional, adjust to taste)
- 1 can (14 ounces) diced tomatoes
- 1 can (14 ounces) chickpeas, drained and rinsed
- 1 medium carrot, sliced
- 1 medium bell pepper, diced
- 1 cup cauliflower florets
- 1 cup broccoli florets
- 1 cup coconut milk
- Salt and black pepper to taste
- Fresh cilantro, chopped (for garnish)

Directions:

1. In a medium-sized saucepan, combine the brown rice and water. After bringing the mixture to a boiling point, lower the heat to a gentle simmer. Place a lid on the saucepan and let the rice simmer for approximately 20-25 minutes until it becomes tender and absorbs all the water. Remove from heat and let it rest for a few minutes.
2. In a large skillet or pot, heat the vegetable oil over medium heat.

3. Introduce the chopped onion to the skillet and sauté it for about 2-3 minutes until it turns translucent.

4. Incorporate the minced garlic and grated ginger into the mixture. Let the ingredients cook for an extra minute until their delightful aromas are fully released.

5. Incorporate the curry powder, ground cumin, ground turmeric, and cayenne pepper (if desired). Stir thoroughly to ensure that the onions and spices are evenly coated.

6. Incorporate the diced tomatoes, including their juice, into the mixture. Stir thoroughly and allow it to simmer for a duration of 5 minutes.

7. Add the drained and rinsed chickpeas, sliced carrot, diced bell pepper, cauliflower florets, and broccoli florets to the skillet. Stir to combine all the ingredients.

8. Integrate the coconut milk into the mixture and customize the seasoning by adding salt and black pepper according to your individual preferences. Thoroughly stir all the ingredients together.

9. Cover the skillet and simmer for 10-15 minutes, or until the vegetables are tender but still have a slight crunch.

10. While the curry is simmering, fluff the cooked brown rice with a fork.

11. Divide the brown rice into two serving bowls or plates.

12. Spoon the vegetable and chickpea curry over the brown rice.

13. Garnish with fresh chopped cilantro.

14. Serve the aromatic and satisfying vegetable and chickpea curry with brown rice as a delicious meal for two.

Nutritional breakdown per serving:

Calories: 450-500 kcal, Protein: 14 grams, Carbohydrates: 70 grams, Fat: 15 grams, Saturated Fat: 8 grams, Cholesterol: 0 milligrams, Sodium: 800 milligrams, Fiber: 12 grams, and Sugar: 8 grams.

QUINOA AND ROASTED VEGETABLE MEDLEY

- Prep Time: 15 minutes
- Total Cooking Time: 35 minutes
- Servings: 2

Ingredients:

- 1 cup quinoa
- 2 cups vegetable broth or water
- 1 small zucchini, sliced
- 1 small yellow squash, sliced
- 1 red bell pepper, sliced
- 1 small red onion, sliced
- 2 tablespoons olive oil
- 2 cloves garlic, minced
- 1 teaspoon dried thyme
- 1/2 teaspoon dried rosemary
- Salt and black pepper to taste
- Juice of 1 lemon
- 2 tablespoons chopped fresh parsley
- Optional toppings: crumbled feta cheese, toasted pine nuts

Directions:

1. Ensure the oven is preheated to 400°F (200°C) before starting your cooking preparations.
2. Rinse the quinoa under cold water and drain well.
3. In a medium saucepan, bring the vegetable broth or water to a boil. Add the rinsed quinoa and simmer, covered, for about 15 minutes until tender and the liquid is absorbed. Take the saucepan off the heat and allow the quinoa to rest for a short period.
4. Next, arrange the zucchini, yellow squash, red bell pepper, and red onion slices evenly onto a baking sheet. Gently pour olive oil over the vegetables and then evenly sprinkle them with minced garlic, dried thyme, dried rosemary, salt, and black pepper. Toss to coat the vegetables evenly.

5. Cook the vegetables in the preheated oven for about 20 minutes, or until they become tender and acquire a gentle browning.

6. Take a large mixing bowl and combine the cooked quinoa and roasted vegetables in it. Gently squeeze the juice of one lemon onto the mixture, and carefully toss it to ensure that all the components are thoroughly blended.

7. If necessary, add more salt and black pepper to season according to your taste preferences.

8. Sprinkle with chopped fresh parsley.

9. Divide the quinoa and roasted vegetable medley into two serving bowls.

10. For an enhanced flavor experience, you can opt to enhance the dish by delicately sprinkling crumbled feta cheese and toasted pine nuts as a delightful garnish.

11. Serve the nutritious and flavorful quinoa and roasted vegetable medley as a wholesome meal for two.

Nutritional breakdown per serving:

Calories: 350-400 kcal, Protein: 10 grams, Carbohydrates: 50 grams, Fat: 15 grams, Saturated Fat: 2 grams, Cholesterol: 0 milligrams, Sodium: 600 milligrams, Fiber: 8 grams, and Sugar: 6 grams.

SPAGHETTI SQUASH WITH PESTO AND ROASTED TOMATOES

- Prep Time: 15 minutes
- Total Cooking Time: 45 minutes
- Servings: 2

Ingredients:

- 1 medium spaghetti squash
- 2 tablespoons olive oil, divided
- Salt and black pepper to taste
- 1 cup cherry tomatoes, halved
- 1/4 cup pine nuts
- 2 cups fresh basil leaves
- 2 cloves garlic, minced
- 1/4 cup grated Parmesan cheese
- Juice of 1/2 lemon
- Optional garnish: fresh basil leaves, grated Parmesan cheese

Directions:

1. Ensure the oven is preheated to 400°F (200°C) before starting your cooking preparations.
2. Simply cut the spaghetti squash in half lengthwise from stem to end. Then, scoop out the seeds and fibrous pulp from the center cavity.
3. Lightly coat the insides of the halved spaghetti squash with 1 tablespoon of olive oil. Don't forget to sprinkle them with salt and black pepper for extra flavor.
4. Put the spaghetti squash halves on a baking sheet, with the cut flesh facing downwards. Place the prepared ingredients in the preheated oven and allow them to roast for approximately 35-40 minutes, or until the flesh becomes tender and can be effortlessly pulled apart into strands using a fork.
5. While the spaghetti squash cooks in the oven, prepare the roasted tomatoes. Coat halved cherry tomatoes with olive oil, salt, and black pepper. Bake the tomatoes on a sheet for 15-20 minutes until they blister and caramelize.

6. Warm a skillet over medium heat and toast the nuts until they turn golden brown. Alternatively, you can achieve the same effect by tossing pine nuts in a hot skillet until they become golden.

7. In a food processor or blender, combine the fresh basil leaves, minced garlic, toasted pine nuts, grated Parmesan cheese (if using), lemon juice, and a pinch of salt and black pepper. Pulse until the mixture is well combined and forms a coarse paste. If needed, drizzle in a little olive oil to achieve desired consistency.

8. When the squash is cooked, use a fork to gently scrape and shred the flesh into spaghetti-like strands.

9. Toss the spaghetti squash strands into a large mixing bowl. Add the pesto sauce and roasted tomatoes. Toss gently to coat the spaghetti squash evenly.

10. Divide the spaghetti squash mixture into two serving plates or bowls.

11. Fresh basil leaves and grated Parmesan cheese make a lovely finishing touch.

12. Serve the delicious and vibrant spaghetti squash with pesto and roasted tomatoes as a satisfying meal for two.

Nutritional breakdown per serving:
Calories: 300-350 kcal, Protein: 10 grams, Carbohydrates: 50 grams, Fat: 15 grams, Saturated Fat: 2 grams, Cholesterol: 0 milligrams, Sodium: 200 milligrams, Fiber: 6 grams, and Sugar: 8 grams.

BROWN RICE BOWL WITH TERIYAKI VEGETABLES

- Prep Time: 15 minutes
- Total Cooking Time: 30 minutes
- Servings: 2

Ingredients:
- 1 cup brown rice
- 2 cups water
- 2 tablespoons soy sauce
- 2 tablespoons honey
- 2 tablespoons rice vinegar
- 1 tablespoon sesame oil
- 2 cloves garlic, minced
- 1 tablespoon grated ginger
- 1 small onion, sliced
- 1 medium bell pepper, sliced
- 1 medium carrot, julienned
- 1 cup broccoli florets
- 1 cup snap peas, trimmed
- Optional garnish: sesame seeds, sliced green onions

Directions:
1. Rinse the brown rice under cold water and drain well.
2. Begin by rinsing the rice in a fine-mesh strainer under cold running water, ensuring a thorough rinse. Continue rinsing until the water runs clear. This process effectively removes any surplus starch that may cause the cooked rice to become sticky. Remove from heat and let it rest for a few minutes.
3. In a compact bowl, combine the soy sauce, honey, rice vinegar, sesame oil, minced garlic, and grated ginger. Whisk the ingredients together until they form a smooth teriyaki sauce. Set the sauce aside for later use.
4. Place a generously sized skillet or wok on the stovetop over medium-high heat. If needed, you can add a small quantity of oil to the heated pan.

166

5. Introduce the sliced onion to the pan and cook it for approximately 2-3 minutes, or until it achieves a translucent appearance.

6. Add the bell pepper, julienned carrot, broccoli florets, and snap peas to the skillet. Stir-fry for about 5-7 minutes, or until the vegetables are crisp-tender.

7. Carefully drizzle the teriyaki sauce over the vegetables in the skillet, making sure to coat them evenly. Stir the mixture to ensure that the sauce is well distributed, and continue cooking for an additional 1-2 minutes until the sauce slightly thickens.

8. Divide the cooked brown rice into two serving bowls. Top with the teriyaki vegetables.

9. For added crunch and freshness, top with sesame seeds and thinly sliced green onions (optional).

10. Serve the flavorful and nourishing brown rice bowl with teriyaki vegetables as a delicious meal for two.

Nutritional breakdown per serving:

Calories: 400-450 kcal, Protein: 10 grams, Carbohydrates: 80 grams, Fat: 8 grams, Saturated Fat: 1 grams, Cholesterol: 0 milligrams, Sodium: 900 milligrams, Fiber: 10 grams, and Sugar: 16 grams.

CHAPTER 5
DESSERTS

BAKED APPLES WITH CINNAMON

- Prep Time: 10 minutes
- Total Cooking Time: 40 minutes
- Servings: 2

Ingredients:

- 2 medium-sized apples (such as Granny Smith or Honeycrisp)
- 2 tablespoons melted butter (vegan: coconut oil)
- 2 tablespoons brown sugar (coconut sugar for reduced sweetness)
- 1 teaspoon ground cinnamon
- Optional toppings: vanilla ice cream, whipped cream, chopped nuts

Directions:

1. Creating an optimal cooking environment begins with the first step of preheating the oven to 375°F (190°C).
2. Extract the core from the apples using either an apple corer or a small knife, being careful to preserve the bottom of the apples.
3. In a small bowl, mix together the melted butter, brown sugar, and ground cinnamon until well combined.
4. Move the apples with the cores removed to either a baking dish or a sheet pan.
5. Spoon the cinnamon mixture into the hollowed-out centers of the apples, distributing it evenly.
6. If there is any remaining cinnamon mixture, drizzle it over the tops of the apples.
7. Place the apples in the preheated oven and bake them for approximately 30-35 minutes, or until they reach a tender texture and the cinnamon mixture becomes caramelized.
8. Take out the baked apples from the oven and allow them to cool for a short while.
9. Serve the warm baked apples as they are or with optional toppings like vanilla ice cream, whipped cream, or chopped nuts.
10. Enjoy the delightful and comforting baked apples with cinnamon as a sweet treat for two.

Nutritional breakdown per serving:
Calories: 180-200 kcal, Protein: 0 grams, Carbohydrates: 30 grams, Fat: 8 grams, Saturated Fat: 5 grams, Cholesterol: 20 milligrams, Sodium: 0 milligrams, Fiber: 4 grams, and Sugar: 24 grams.

MIXED BERRY PARFAIT

- Prep Time: 15 minutes
- Total Cooking Time: 0 minutes (No cooking required)
- Servings: 2

Ingredients:
- 1 cup Greek yogurt (plain or vanilla-flavored)
- 1 tablespoon honey (optional)
- 1 cup berries (strawberries, blueberries, raspberries)
- 1/4 cup granola
- Optional toppings: mint leaves, shredded coconut, a drizzle of chocolate sauce

Directions:

1. Set aside the Greek yogurt and honey (if desired) mixture in a small bowl after thoroughly combining them.
2. Rinse the mixed berries under cold water and pat them dry with a paper towel. Slice the strawberries if desired.
3. Prepare two serving glasses or bowls.
4. Begin layering the parfait by adding a spoonful of Greek yogurt to the bottom of each glass.
5. On top of the yogurt, create a layer of mixed berries, and then sprinkle a generous amount of granola.
6. Continue layering the ingredients until the glasses are filled, concluding with a final dollop of Greek yogurt placed on the very top.
7. Garnish the parfaits with additional mixed berries, mint leaves, shredded coconut, or a drizzle of chocolate sauce, if desired.
8. Serve the refreshing and indulgent mixed berry parfait immediately.

Nutritional breakdown per serving:
Calories: 200-250 kcal, Protein: 12 grams, Carbohydrates: 30 grams, Fat: 5 grams, Saturated Fat: 1 grams, Cholesterol: 10 milligrams, Sodium: 45 milligrams, Fiber: 4 grams, and Sugar: 20 grams.

DARK CHOCOLATE-DIPPED STRAWBERRIES

- Prep Time: 15 minutes
- Total Cooking Time: 10 minutes (plus chilling time)
- Servings: 2

Ingredients:

- 8-10 fresh strawberries
- 3 ounces dark chocolate, chopped
- Optional toppings: chopped nuts, shredded coconut, sprinkles

Directions:

1. To be ready for later use, set aside a baking sheet and take the time to prepare it by lining it with either parchment paper or wax paper.
2. To prepare the strawberries for dipping, rinse them under cold water and gently pat them dry using a paper towel. It is recommended to leave the stems intact to facilitate the dipping process.
3. In a microwave-safe bowl, melt the dark chocolate in the microwave in 30-second intervals, stirring well in between each interval until smooth and fully melted. Alternatively, you can melt the chocolate using a double boiler on the stovetop.
4. For melted chocolate, microwave chopped dark chocolate in a microwave-safe bowl in 30-second bursts. Stir the chocolate well between each interval until it becomes smooth and completely melted. If preferred, an alternative method to melt the chocolate is by using a double boiler on the stovetop.
5. For even coating, dip strawberries by the stem, twisting slightly in the melted chocolate. Allow any excess chocolate to drip off.
6. Place the chocolate-coated strawberry on the prepared baking sheet. Repeat the process with the remaining strawberries.
7. If desired, while the chocolate is still wet, sprinkle the dipped strawberries with chopped nuts, shredded coconut, or sprinkles for added flavor and decoration.
8. Once dipped and decorated, refrigerate the strawberries on a baking sheet for 30 minutes, or until chocolate sets.
9. After chilling, the dark chocolate-dipped strawberries are ready to be served.

Nutritional breakdown per serving:

Calories: 100-150 kcal, Protein: 1 grams, Carbohydrates: 12 grams, Fat: 7 grams, Saturated Fat: 4 grams, Cholesterol: 0 milligrams, Sodium: 0 milligrams, Fiber: 2 grams, and Sugar: 8 grams.

CHIA SEED PUDDING

- Prep Time: 5 minutes (plus chilling time)
- Total Cooking Time: 0 minutes
- Servings: 2

Ingredients:
- 1/4 cup chia seeds
- 1 cup milk of your choice
- 1-2 tablespoons sweetener of your choice (such as honey, maple syrup, or agave syrup)
- 1/2 teaspoon vanilla extract
- Fresh fruits, nuts, or granola for topping (optional)

Directions:
1. For the pudding, mix chia seeds, milk, sweetener, and vanilla extract in a bowl. Ensure the chia seeds and sweetener are well combined.
2. Rest for 5 minutes, then whisk again to disperse any chia seed clumps.
3. For storage, either cover the bowl with plastic wrap or transfer the mixture to individual jars or glasses. Refrigerate at least 2 hours, or overnight, for the chia seeds to hydrate and set into pudding.
4. After chilling, give the chia seed pudding a good stir to ensure it is evenly thickened.
5. If desired, serve the chia seed pudding as is or top it with fresh fruits, nuts, or granola for added texture and flavor.
6. Enjoy this nutritious chia seed pudding! This creamy dessert, perfect for two, makes a satisfying breakfast or a delightful post-dinner treat.

Nutritional breakdown per serving:
Calories: 150-200 kcal, Protein: 5 grams, Carbohydrates: 15 grams, Fat: 9 grams, Saturated Fat: 1 grams, Cholesterol: 0 milligrams, Sodium: 50 milligrams, Fiber: 10 grams, and Sugar: 5 grams.

GREEK YOGURT WITH HONEY AND NUTS

- Prep Time: 5 minutes
- Total Cooking Time: 0 minutes
- Servings: 2

Ingredients:

- 1 cup Greek yogurt
- 2 tablespoons honey (adjust to taste)
- 1/4 cup chopped almonds, walnuts, and pistachios
- Optional toppings: fresh berries, granola, or a sprinkle of cinnamon

Directions:

1. Before grilling, ensure that the grill or grill pan is preheated to medium-high heat.
2. Drizzle the honey over the Greek yogurt, adjusting the amount to your desired level of sweetness.
3. Sprinkle the chopped nuts over the yogurt and honey, distributing them evenly.
4. For additional flavor and texture, consider adding optional toppings such as fresh berries, granola, or a dash of cinnamon, according to your preference.
5. Serve the Greek yogurt with honey and nuts immediately, or refrigerate for a short time if you prefer a chilled dessert or snack.

Nutritional breakdown per serving:

Calories: 200-250 kcal, Protein: 15 grams, Carbohydrates: 20 grams, Fat: 10 grams, Saturated Fat: 2 grams, Cholesterol: 10 milligrams, Sodium: 60 milligrams, Fiber: 2 grams, and Sugar: 15 grams.

GRILLED PINEAPPLE WITH MINT

- Prep Time: 10 minutes
- Total Cooking Time: 10 minutes
- Servings: 2

Ingredients:

- 1 ripe pineapple
- 2 tablespoons honey
- 1 tablespoon fresh mint leaves, chopped
- Optional toppings: vanilla ice cream or Greek yogurt

Directions:

1. Before grilling, ensure that the grill or grill pan is preheated to medium-high heat.
2. Slice off the top and bottom of the pineapple, then remove the outer skin with a sharp knife.
3. Prepare the pineapple by slicing it into rings or spears, with each slice being approximately 1/2 inch thick.
4. In a small bowl, mix together the honey and chopped mint leaves.
5. Ensure both sides of the pineapple slices are evenly coated by brushing them with the honey and mint mixture.
6. Position the pineapple slices on the grill or grill pan that has been preheated, and cook them for approximately 4-5 minutes on each side. Keep an eye out for the formation of grill marks and a slight caramelization of the pineapple slices.
7. Remove the grilled pineapple from the heat and transfer them to a serving plate.
8. The grilled pineapple can be served as is or used as a side dish. Enhance the dessert experience by adding a delightful touch to the grilled pineapple with a scoop of velvety vanilla ice cream or a dollop of tangy Greek yogurt as an exquisite topping.
9. Garnish with additional mint leaves, if desired.
10. Savor the sweet-tart tango of grilled pineapple with a burst of fresh garden mint.

Nutritional breakdown per serving:

Calories: 150-200 kcal, Protein: 1 grams, Carbohydrates: 40 grams, Fat: 1 grams, Saturated Fat: 0 grams, Cholesterol: 0 milligrams, Sodium: 0 milligrams, Fiber: 4 grams, and Sugar: 30 grams.

BAKED PEARS WITH ALMONDS

- Prep Time: 10 minutes
- Total Cooking Time: 30 minutes
- Servings: 2

Ingredients:

- 2 ripe pears
- 2 tablespoons unsalted butter, melted
- 2 tablespoons honey
- 1/4 teaspoon ground cinnamon
- 1/4 cup sliced almonds

Directions:

1. To ensure ideal cooking conditions, start by preheating the oven to 375°F (190°C).
2. Cut the pears in half from top to bottom. Use a spoon or melon baller to remove the cores, leaving a small hollow in each half.
3. Place the pear halves cut-side up in a baking dish.
4. Make the topping by whisking melted butter, honey, and cinnamon together in a small bowl.
5. Drizzle the honey and butter mixture evenly over the pear halves, ensuring they are well coated.
6. Sprinkle the sliced almonds on top of the pears, pressing them gently into the honey and butter mixture.
7. Pop the covered dish in the preheated oven for 20 minutes, and voila! A perfectly cooked dish awaits.
8. Bake covered for 20 minutes. For tender pears and golden brown almonds, remove the foil and bake for an additional 5-10 minutes, checking for desired doneness.
9. Take the baked pears out of the oven and let them rest for 5-10 minutes. This allows them to cool slightly and settle for perfect serving.
10. Serve the baked pears warm as a delicious dessert or snack.

Nutritional breakdown per serving:

Calories: 220-250 kcal, Protein: 3 grams, Carbohydrates: 30 grams, Fat: 12 grams, Saturated Fat: 4 grams, Cholesterol: 15 milligrams, Sodium: 0 milligrams, Fiber: 5 grams, and Sugar: 20 grams.

BANANA NICE CREAM

- Prep Time: 5 minutes (plus freezing time)
- Total Cooking Time: 0 minutes
- Servings: 2

Ingredients:

- 3 ripe bananas, peeled and sliced
- 2 tablespoons nut butter (almond, peanut, cashew)
- Optional toppings: chopped nuts, shredded coconut, chocolate chips, or fresh fruit slices

Directions:

1. Spread the sliced bananas evenly in a single layer on a baking sheet that has been lined with parchment paper or a silicone mat.
2. Transfer the baking sheet with the bananas to the freezer and allow them to freeze for a minimum of 2 hours, or until they are completely solidified.
3. After the bananas have been frozen, proceed to transfer them into a high-speed blender or a food processor.
4. Introduce your preferred nut butter to the frozen bananas.
5. Blend the bananas and nut butter together until smooth and creamy, scraping down the sides as needed. This may take a few minutes and will require stopping and starting the blender or food processor several times.
6. When the mixture achieves a smooth and velvety texture, it is prepared and can be served immediately.
7. Scoop the banana nice cream into bowls or glasses.
8. If desired, top the banana nice cream with chopped nuts, shredded coconut, chocolate chips, or fresh fruit slices for added texture and flavor.
9. Serve the banana nice cream immediately and enjoy its natural sweetness and creamy texture as a healthy and refreshing dessert or snack.

Nutritional breakdown per serving:

Calories: 150-200 kcal, Protein: 3 grams, Carbohydrates: 30 grams, Fat: 5 grams, Saturated Fat: 1 grams, Cholesterol: 0 milligrams, Sodium: 0 milligrams, Fiber: 4 grams, and Sugar: 15 grams.

STRAWBERRY AND SPINACH SALAD

- Prep Time: 10 minutes
- Total Cooking Time: 0 minutes
- Servings: 2

Ingredients:

- 4 cups fresh baby spinach leaves
- 1 cup fresh strawberries, sliced
- 1/4 cup red onion, thinly sliced
- 1/4 cup crumbled feta cheese
- 1/4 cup sliced almonds
- Protein option: grilled chicken or shrimp

For the Dressing:

- 2 tablespoons balsamic vinegar
- 1 tablespoon extra-virgin olive oil
- 1 teaspoon honey
- Salt and pepper to taste

Directions:

1. In a spacious salad bowl, bring together the baby spinach, sliced strawberries, red onion, crumbled feta cheese, and sliced almonds. Give them a gentle toss until they are thoroughly mixed and blended.
2. To enhance the protein content, you have the option of including grilled chicken or shrimp in the salad, should you wish to do so.
3. Mix together the balsamic vinegar, olive oil, honey, salt, and pepper in a small bowl, whisking until the ingredients are fully combined.
4. Pour the dressing over the salad, allowing it to drizzle evenly, then gently toss the ingredients to ensure they are coated uniformly.
5. Serve the strawberry and spinach salad immediately as a refreshing and nutritious meal for two.

Nutritional breakdown per serving:
Calories: 200-250 kcal, Protein: 8 grams, Carbohydrates: 15 grams, Fat: 15 grams, Saturated Fat: 4 grams, Cholesterol: 15 milligrams, Sodium: 250 milligrams, Fiber: 4 grams, and Sugar: 8 grams.

FRUIT KABOBS WITH YOGURT DIP

- Prep Time: 15 minutes
- Total Cooking Time: 0 minutes
- Servings: 2

Ingredients:

- 1 cup strawberries, hulled and halved
- 1 cup pineapple chunks
- 1 cup grapes
- 1 banana, sliced
- 1 cup plain Greek yogurt
- 1 tablespoon honey (optional)
- Skewers or toothpicks for assembling the kabobs

Directions:

1. Get the fruit ready by washing them thoroughly and then cutting them into bite-sized pieces.
2. Thread the fruit onto skewers or toothpicks, alternating between different fruits to create colorful combinations.
3. If desired, combine Greek yogurt with honey in a small bowl to create a smooth and sweet dip.
4. Arrange the fruit kabobs on a serving platter.
5. Serve the fruit kabobs with the yogurt dip on the side, allowing each person to dip their fruit kabobs into the yogurt as desired.
6. Enjoy the refreshing and healthy fruit kabobs with the creamy yogurt dip as a delightful snack or dessert.

Nutritional breakdown per serving:

Calories: 150-200 kcal, Protein: 10 grams, Carbohydrates: 35 grams, Fat: 1 grams, Saturated Fat: 0 grams, Cholesterol: 5 milligrams, Sodium: 40 milligrams, Fiber: 4 grams, and Sugar: 25 grams.

BAKED CINNAMON-SPICED PEACHES

- Prep Time: 10 minutes
- Total Cooking Time: 20 minutes
- Servings: 2

Ingredients:

- 2 ripe peaches
- 2 tablespoons unsalted butter, melted
- 1 tablespoon honey
- 1/2 teaspoon ground cinnamon
- Ice cream or whip (optional)

Directions:

1. To ensure ideal cooking conditions, start by preheating the oven to 375°F (190°C).
2. Halve the peaches and remove the pits. Fill a baking dish with the peach halves, cut-side up, showcasing their beautiful golden flesh.
3. Honey, melted butter, and a touch of cinnamon - simply whisk them together in a small bowl for a tasty topping.
4. Drizzle the honey and cinnamon mixture evenly over the peach halves, making sure they are well coated.
5. Nestle the baking dish filled with peaches in the preheated oven. In about 15-20 minutes, they'll be tender and caramelized - a sign they're perfect!
6. Take out the baked peaches from the oven and allow them to cool for a few minutes.
7. Pamper yourself with a delightful dessert by savoring the warm baked peaches, either on their own or paired with a scoop of smooth, velvety vanilla ice cream or a heavenly dollop of whipped cream.
8. Enjoy the sweet and fragrant flavors of the baked cinnamon-spiced peaches.

Nutritional breakdown per serving:

Calories: 150-200 kcal, Protein: 1 grams, Carbohydrates: 22 grams, Fat: 8 grams, Saturated Fat: 5 grams, Cholesterol: 20 milligrams, Sodium: 0 milligrams, Fiber: 3 grams, and Sugar: 19 grams.

MANGO SORBET

- Prep Time: 10 minutes (plus freezing time)
- Total Cooking Time: 0 minutes
- Servings: 2

Ingredients:

- 2 ripe mangoes, peeled and pitted
- 2 tablespoons fresh lime juice
- 2 tablespoons honey (or sweetener of your choice)
- Optional garnish: fresh mint leaves or sliced mangoes

Directions:

1. Separate the mango flesh from the pit by cutting it and then transfer the mango into a blender or food processor.
2. Toss the fresh lime juice and honey into your blender or food processor.
3. Give it a good whirl until everything is perfectly combined. Take breaks to scrape down the sides for a flawless consistency.
4. After achieving a smooth texture, evaluate the sweetness of the mixture and make any desired adjustments by adding additional honey to achieve the desired level of sweetness.
5. Pour the mango mixture into a shallow, freezer-safe container. Secure the container by covering it with a lid or tightly sealing it with plastic wrap.
6. Place the container in the freezer and let it freeze for at least 4 hours or until firm.
7. After the mango mixture has been frozen, take it out of the freezer and allow it to sit at room temperature for a few minutes, enabling it to soften slightly.
8. Transfer the partially softened sorbet to a blender or food processor and blend again until smooth and creamy.
9. Return the sorbet to the freezer container and freeze for another 2 hours or until firm.
10. Serve the mango sorbet in bowls or glasses, garnished with fresh mint leaves or sliced mangoes if desired.
11. Enjoy the refreshing and naturally sweet mango sorbet as a delightful dessert or treat.

Nutritional breakdown per serving:
Calories: 150-200 kcal, Protein: 2 grams, Carbohydrates: 38 grams, Fat: 1 grams, Saturated Fat: 0 grams, Cholesterol: 0 milligrams, Sodium: 5 milligrams, Fiber: 3 grams, and Sugar: 35 grams.

ROASTED PLUMS WITH GREEK YOGURT

- Prep Time: 10 minutes
- Total Cooking Time: 25 minutes
- Servings: 2

Ingredients:

- 4 ripe plums, halved and pitted
- 1 tablespoon honey
- 1/2 teaspoon ground cinnamon
- 1 cup Greek yogurt
- Optional toppings: chopped nuts, granola, or a drizzle of honey

Directions:

1. To ensure ideal cooking conditions, start by preheating the oven to 375°F (190°C).
2. Place the halved and pitted plums on a baking sheet, cut-side up.
3. Drizzle the plums with honey and sprinkle them with ground cinnamon.
4. Allow the plums to rest in the preheated oven for around 20 to 25 minutes until they reach a tender consistency and acquire a delicate caramelization.
5. While the plums are roasting, divide the Greek yogurt equally between two serving bowls or glasses.
6. Once the plums are done, remove them from the oven and let them cool slightly.
7. Place two roasted plum halves on top of each serving of Greek yogurt.
8. If desired, garnish the roasted plums and Greek yogurt with chopped nuts, granola, or a drizzle of honey.
9. Serve the roasted plums with Greek yogurt immediately as a delicious and healthy dessert or breakfast.

Nutritional breakdown per serving:

Calories: 150-200 kcal, Protein: 10 grams, Carbohydrates: 30 grams, Fat: 2 grams, Saturated Fat: 1 grams, Cholesterol: 5 milligrams, Sodium: 20 milligrams, Fiber: 3 grams, and Sugar: 25 grams.

BLUEBERRY OATMEAL BARS

- Prep Time: 15 minutes
- Total Cooking Time: 40 minutes
- Servings: 2

Ingredients:

- 1 cup rolled oats
- 1/2 cup all-purpose flour
- 1/4 cup brown sugar
- 1/4 teaspoon baking powder
- 1/4 teaspoon salt
- 1/4 cup unsalted butter, melted
- 1/2 teaspoon vanilla extract
- 1 cup fresh or frozen blueberries
- 1 tablespoon lemon juice
- Optional: powdered sugar for dusting

Directions:

1. To ensure ideal cooking conditions, start by preheating the oven to 350°F (175°C). Prepare a small baking dish by either greasing it or lining it with parchment paper.
2. Grab a mixing bowl (or a large container if you're doubling the recipe). In there, combine the rolled oats, all-purpose flour, brown sugar, baking powder, and salt.
3. Drizzle the melted butter and vanilla extract over the dry ingredients in the mixing bowl.
4. Keep aside a dedicated portion of the dough, approximately 1/2 cup, specifically for crafting the topping. Proceed by gently pressing the remaining dough into the bottom of the baking dish that has been prepared, forming a sturdy and uniform crust.
5. In a different bowl, combine the blueberries with lemon juice, ensuring they are well coated. Proceed to evenly distribute the blueberries over the prepared crust.
6. Sprinkle the reserved dough evenly over the blueberries as a crumbly topping.
7. Gently transfer the baking dish into the preheated oven and allow it to bake for approximately 25 to 30 minutes, or until the edges acquire a delightful golden brown shade and the blueberries start to bubble with an inviting charm.

8. Remove from the oven and let the blueberry oatmeal bars cool in the baking dish for a few minutes.

9. After the bars have cooled down, delicately lift them out of the dish and transfer them onto a cutting board. Proceed to cut them into squares or rectangles, as desired.

10. For an optional decorative touch, sprinkle a light dusting of powdered sugar over the bars.For an optional decorative touch, you can sprinkle some powdered sugar over the bars.

11. Serve the blueberry oatmeal bars as a delicious breakfast or snack for two.

Nutritional breakdown per serving:

Calories: 250-300 kcal, Protein: 4 grams, Carbohydrates: 37 grams, Fat: 11 grams, Saturated Fat: 6 grams, Cholesterol: 25 milligrams, Sodium: 120 milligrams, Fiber: 3 grams, and Sugar: 16 grams.

WATERMELON AND MINT SALAD

- Prep Time: 10 minutes
- Total Cooking Time: 0 minutes
- Servings: 2

Ingredients:

- 3 cups cubed seedless watermelon
- 1/4 cup fresh mint leaves, chopped
- 2 tablespoons fresh lime juice
- 1 tablespoon honey
- 1/4 cup crumbled feta cheese (optional)
- Optional garnish: extra mint leaves for garnish

Directions:

1. Toss them together in a large bowl. The vibrant mix of colors and the refreshing scent promise a delightful summer treat.
2. In a small bowl, whisk these two ingredients together until everything is perfectly incorporated.
3. Drizzle the tangy lime-honey mixture over them, then gently toss everything together to ensure each juicy watermelon cube gets a delightful flavor kiss.
4. For added flavor, you have the option to scatter the crumbled feta cheese over the salad and give it a gentle toss once more.
5. Let the watermelon and mint salad sit for a few minutes to allow the flavors to meld together.
6. Garnish with extra mint leaves, if desired, before serving.
7. Serve the watermelon and mint salad as a refreshing side dish or light dessert for two.

Nutritional breakdown per serving:
Calories: 100-150 kcal, Protein: 1 grams, Carbohydrates: 25 grams, Fat: 1 grams, Saturated Fat: 0 grams, Cholesterol: 0 milligrams, Sodium: 30 milligrams, Fiber: 1 grams, and Sugar: 20 grams.

BAKED CINNAMON-SUGAR TORTILLA CHIPS

- Prep Time: 10 minutes
- Total Cooking Time: 12 minutes
- Servings: 2

Ingredients:

- 4 small flour tortillas
- 2 tablespoons unsalted butter, melted
- 2 tablespoons granulated sugar
- 1 teaspoon ground cinnamon
- Optional: fruit salsa or sweet dip for serving

Directions:

1. To ensure ideal cooking conditions, start by preheating the oven to 350°F (175°C).
2. Stack the tortillas and cut them into wedges, like you would cut a pizza.
3. In a small bowl, create your cinnamon sugar magic by whisking the granulated sugar and ground cinnamon together.
4. Using a pastry brush (or a spoon in a pinch), generously coat both sides of each tortilla wedge with the melted butter.
5. After coating the tortilla wedges with butter, generously dredge them in the cinnamon sugar mixture, ensuring both sides are evenly coated.
6. Place the coated tortilla wedges in a single layer on a baking sheet.
7. Pop the tortilla wedges in the preheated oven and bake for 10-12 minutes. Aim for crispy and lightly golden chips.
8. Once golden brown, remove the tortilla chips from the oven and let them crisp up further on the baking sheet for a few minutes.
9. Serve the baked cinnamon-sugar tortilla chips as a delicious snack or dessert for two.
10. Optionally, pair them with fruit salsa or a sweet dip of your choice.

Nutritional breakdown per serving:

Calories: 150-200 kcal, Protein: 2 grams, Carbohydrates: 20 grams, Fat: 8 grams, Saturated Fat: 4 grams, Cholesterol: 15 milligrams, Sodium: 150 milligrams, Fiber: 1 grams, and Sugar: 8 grams.

FROZEN GRAPES

- Prep Time: 5 minutes
- Total Cooking Time: 0 minutes
- Servings: 2

Ingredients:

- 2 cups seedless grapes (red, green, or a mix)
- Optional: wooden skewers

Directions:

1. Give the grapes a good rinse by holding them under running water. After rinsing, gently dab the grapes with a paper towel to remove excess moisture.
2. If desired, thread the grapes onto wooden skewers for easy handling. For a more organized freeze, thread grapes onto skewers. Loose freezing is also possible!
3. Spread the grapes out on a parchment-lined or silicone baking sheet, leaving space between each one, regardless of whether you used skewers.
4. Pop the baking sheet with the grapes (loose or skewered) into the freezer and let them freeze for at least 2 hours, or until they're solid and icy.
5. When the grapes are frozen through, remove the baking sheet from the freezer. To prevent freezer burn, transfer the frozen grapes to a resealable bag or airtight container.
6. Store the frozen grapes in the freezer until ready to serve.
7. To serve:
8. Take the desired number of frozen grapes out of the freezer and let them sit at room temperature for a few minutes to slightly soften.
9. Remove the grapes from the skewers, if using.
10. Serve the frozen grapes as a refreshing and naturally sweet snack for two.

Nutritional breakdown per serving:

Calories: 60-80 kcal, Protein: 1 grams, Carbohydrates: 15 grams, Fat: 0 grams, Saturated Fat: 0 grams, Cholesterol: 0 milligrams, Sodium: 0 milligrams, Fiber: 1 grams, and Sugar: 14 grams.

PINEAPPLE COCONUT CHIA PUDDING

- Prep Time: 10 minutes
- Total Cooking Time: 4 hours (including chilling time)
- Servings: 2

Ingredients:

- 1 cup coconut milk
- 1/4 cup chia seeds
- 1 tablespoon honey or maple syrup
- 1/2 teaspoon vanilla extract
- 1/2 cup diced pineapple
- Optional toppings: shredded coconut, sliced almonds, or fresh mint leaves

Directions:

1. Grab a mixing bowl and toss in the coconut milk, chia seeds, honey (or maple syrup, if you prefer), and vanilla extract. Now, get stirring! Make sure there are no pockets of lonely chia seeds and everything is well incorporated.
2. Let the mixture sit for 5 minutes, then give it another stir to prevent clumping.
3. Once everything's well-combined, give the bowl a snug cover and pop it in the fridge. The chia seeds will work their magic, absorbing the liquid for at least 4 hours, or ideally overnight, to achieve that perfect pudding texture.
4. After the chilling time, remove the chia pudding from the refrigerator and give it a good stir to break up any clumps.
5. Divide the chia pudding equally between two serving glasses or bowls.
6. Top each serving with the diced pineapple and any desired optional toppings, such as shredded coconut, sliced almonds, or fresh mint leaves.
7. Serve the pineapple coconut chia pudding immediately as a healthy and satisfying breakfast or dessert for two.

Nutritional breakdown per serving:

Calories: 200-250 kcal, Protein: 4 grams, Carbohydrates: 18 grams, Fat: 15 grams, Saturated Fat: 11 grams, Cholesterol: 0 milligrams, Sodium: 10 milligrams, Fiber: 8 grams, and Sugar: 8 grams.

RASPBERRY YOGURT POPSICLES

- Prep Time: 10 minutes
- Total Cooking Time: 4-6 hours (including freezing time)
- Servings: 2

Ingredients:
- 1 cup fresh or frozen raspberries
- 1 cup plain or vanilla yogurt
- 2 tablespoons honey or maple syrup
- 1/2 teaspoon vanilla extract

Directions:
1. Grab your blender or food processor and load it up with the raspberries, yogurt, honey (or maple syrup, if you prefer), and vanilla extract. Blend it all up until you have a smooth and creamy mixture.
2. Blend everything together until you achieve a smooth and creamy consistency. Give it a taste! If you crave more sweetness, feel free to adjust it by adding a drizzle of honey or maple syrup.
3. Fill your popsicle molds with the vibrant raspberry yogurt mixture, leaving a bit of space at the top for expansion during freezing.
4. Pop a popsicle stick straight into the center of each mold, making sure they stand upright.
5. Pop those molds in and let them freeze for at least 4 hours. For rock-solid popsicles, you can freeze them for even longer.
6. To remove the frozen treats, run warm water over the molds for a few seconds. Once the molds are loosened, gently pull on the popsicle sticks to release your frozen treats.
7. Serve the raspberry yogurt popsicles immediately as a refreshing and guilt-free treat for two.

Nutritional breakdown per serving:
Calories: 120-150 kcal, Protein: 5 grams, Carbohydrates: 24 grams, Fat: 2 grams, Saturated Fat: 1 grams, Cholesterol: 10 milligrams, Sodium: 45 milligrams, Fiber: 4 grams, and Sugar: 19 grams.

ALMOND BUTTER AND BANANA BITES

- Prep Time: 10 minutes
- Total Cooking Time: 0 minutes
- Servings: 2

Ingredients:

- 1 large banana, cut into thick slices
- 2 tablespoons almond butter
- Optional toppings: shredded coconut, chopped nuts, chocolate chips, or honey

Directions:

1. Lay the banana slices flat on a plate or cutting board.
2. Spread almond butter on one side of each banana slice.
3. If desired, sprinkle optional toppings such as shredded coconut, chopped nuts, or chocolate chips over the almond butter.
4. For added sweetness, drizzle a small amount of honey over the banana slices.
5. Gently press another banana slice on top of the almond butter and toppings to create a bite-sized sandwich.
6. Continue this process with the rest of the banana slices until you have a total of 2 delicious almond butter and banana bites!
7. Serve the almond butter and banana bites immediately as a nutritious and satisfying snack for two.

Nutritional breakdown per serving:

Calories: 150-180 kcal, Protein: 4 grams, Carbohydrates: 20 grams, Fat: 8 grams, Saturated Fat: 1 grams, Cholesterol: 0 milligrams, Sodium: 0 milligrams, Fiber: 3 grams, and Sugar: 10 grams.

CONCLUSION

"Heart-Healthy Cookbook for Two" is an exceptionally well-adapted cookbook for couples that search for tasty and nourishing meals that are great for the heart. Providing specific list of foodstuffs suitable for the heart and utilization of proper cooking methods, the cookbook intends to favor the heart health without being boring.

The biggest lesson from this cookbook is that the "cardio healthy" couple's cooking can ensure both your cardio and your marriage so it really doubles your wellbeing. But a balanced diet should include whole food varieties, lean proteins, plant-based fibers as well as healthy fats which will help the couples cut down intake of salt, saturated fats and cholesterols.

Furthermore, this "Heart-Healthy Cookbook for Two" is not only teaching to make better diet choices but also to serve the right size of the portion that if you have excess eating will leads to weight gain and cardiovascular problems. The recipes have been painstakingly calculated to deliver meals that are balanced and adjusted by portions, so that the couples can choose meals that are pleasant and at the same time healthy.

In sum, "Heart-healthy Cookbook for Two" is just a precious selection guide for couples who are willing to start on a way towards a healthy heart- fonction. Engaging in the principle of Healthy eating, portion control and having meal together can help both partners to encouraging and maintain their hearts oneness and have a standing society that is centered on successful wellness.

Made in the USA
Coppell, TX
13 December 2024

42273621R00111